Designing a Zero-Cost Abstraction for Memory-Safe Threading

Jacob

Contents

7 Conclusions and Future Work   69

Chapter 1

Introduction

Embedded devices are increasingly commonplace today. With the advent of Internet of Things (IoT) they will further increase in numbers. As seen in the automotive industry embedded systems are pervasive[1], and this is also true for heavy industry such as mining and manufacturing. The idea behind IoT is that all kind of devices could be connected to Internet.

Embedded devices typically consists of some ARM[2] core coupled with the required peripherals and some means of communication. They are found in mission-critical systems where duties include performing tasks with requirements of real-time and security aspects.

With the increasing demands on functionality and connectivity while still remaining safe and secure, embedded system developers has created tools to aid development. Real-Time Interrupt-driven Concurrency (RTIC) is a Rust implementation of the Real-Time For the Masses (RTFM) [1] framework, enabling deadlock-free multitasking with minimal scheduling overhead. This framework is an execution model which models the system as the familiar concepts of tasks and resources, allowing for extensive analysis and consistency checking of the model at compile time rather than at run-time. Thus the guarantees of race and deadlock free execution and bounded priority inversion are all done before even flashing the hardware. The user is unable to break the assumptions made by the model thanks to the clear separation between safe and unsafe code in Rust.

This thesis aims to report the development of the RTIC framework during this past year, from January 2020 until November 2020. There has been work done in different areas to improve the feature-set, remove limitations and to make RTIC a user friendly but capable contender on the real-time embedded market, both for hobbyists and commercial actors. The intended target audience for this thesis are people interested in embedded development and the emerging possibilities for safer embedded systems thanks to the memory safety guarantees provided by the programming language Rust.

The inner workings of the RTIC framework will be discussed to motivate the improvements beneficial for the user, since being a open-source community driven project the merits and capabilities of the system are what attracts new users. The end goal is to foster a healthy and vibrant community around this framework, ensuring the longevity of the project.

Chapter 1 conveys the background, evolution of the RTFM framework and the outset for this thesis. Chapter 2 discusses related work, approaches towards concurrency on embedded systems. Chapter 3 lays out the theoretical underpinnings and reasoning of the problem at hand while chapter 4 details the implementation. Following that chapter 5 presents the results and chapter 6 provides a discussion of these. Finally, chapter 7 concludes this thesis and proposes what is to come.

1.1 Background

This introductory chapter takes a look into the world of open-source software and its uses in a commercial setting, then the building blocks and evolution of what would become the Real-Time For the Masses framework is introduced.

1.1.1 Open-Source Software (OSS)

The concept of open-source has been around since the early days of creating computer software, notable examples includes Donald Knuth's $T_{\!E}\!X$[3] and Richard Stallman's GNU[4] operating system.

Linus Torvald's Linux[5] is another well known open-source project almost everyone using some sort of computer has in some shape or form interacted with, be it smartphones using the Android operating system or TV set-top boxes, payment terminals, in-flight entertainment systems, web-server backend operating system etc.

The concept of open-source is that the source, primarily program code but can include artwork and documentation among other things, are licensed such that the copyright holder allow anyone to use, study, change and distribute that software to anyone and for any purpose.

More and more companies see the value of the open-source principles and the benefits of using well established and battle-tested software with large user-bases/communities. The notion that software has a large community following indicates that the longevity of the project has stronger guarantees compared with a single developer or even proprietary software which usually stands and falls with the single product owner. The stronger guarantee comes from the ability that if necessary, anyone can take up and continue developing the software.

Open-Source licences

A software licence provides the legal requirements placed on an application and its source-code, governing the copyright and redistribution rights of that software.

There exists a wide swath of various licences used within the concept of open-source. They can be grouped by various metrics, but the primary thing considered is how *permissive* they are.

Some of the more strict licences require that any derivative work **must** also have that same licence, that the original source code must be included as part of the distribution among other things. Notable examples being GPL-2.0[6] and GPL-3.0[7].

The idea is that it should be possible to prevent entities creating proprietary software based on and utilising open-source software without contributing back.

More permissive licences include Apache 2.0[8] and MIT[9]. These are much more relaxed when it comes to what you must do in order to comply, they both require that the original Copyright and Licence is included with any derivative work, Apache 2.0 also requires that changes to the software is indicated and prohibits the use of original

Trademark. For more details see the website tldrlegal.com[10] for a good overview of Apache 2.0[11] and MIT[12] licences.

These are just a few of all available software licences.

It is also possible for the author/copyright holder to double-license their work, meaning that somebody creating a derivative work can at their own discretion pick which of the licences the work adheres to.

1.1.2 Open-Source in commercial products

As discussed in the previous section, the licence dictates what kind of derivative works are possible to create and sell.

Grepit AB[13] designs and develop embedded solutions ranging from custom Application Specific Integrated Circuit (ASIC) to creating the software running on the embedded ARM cores found in Field-Programmable Gate Array (FPGA) like the Xilinx Zynq-7000[14]. A typical requirement is that the system should have real-time properties, meaning that there are deadlines to satisfy in order to achieve correct functionality.

Grepit has been on the forefront testing the emerging Rust programming language both in-house and together with customers within embedded development. With products on the market running Rust and RTIC/RTFM the desire to further enhance the framework becomes apparent. With one of the founders appearing as the first author on the research paper detailing the core concepts which turned into Real-Time For the Masses (RTFM) it becomes clear that Grepit see value in the framework.

Considering that so many components of the software stacks in use today are open-source, and one of the primary ways to enhance open-source apart from financially is by investing time and by furthering development, it makes sense to "give back" to the open-source community.

Notable examples include Red Hat which call themselves "The largest open source company in the world"[15] and their commitment to open-source[16] is motivated by their firm belief that open and transparent solutions leaning on a meritocratic ground results in better[17] software for all.

As an example of how prolific open-source is, starting from the Operating System (OS) a Linux kernel along with GNU core-utils, a whole host of other pieces all being open-source as part of the distribution. The text editor of choice, may it be Vim, Emacs or Visual Studio Code too.

By adhering to the software licence and acting in the interest of the project, a wholesome relation can form where there is mutual benefits for both commercial and open-source parties.

1.1.3 Stack Resource Policy (SRP)

Stack Resource Policy[2] is a method how to handle resource access in real-time systems with a single shared stack. The SRP model fully prevents deadlocks and data races while placing a tight bound on priority inversion. Resources must be locked in a Last-In, First-Out (LIFO) manner and it is also compatible with Earliest Deadline First (EDF) scheduling.

RTFM uses SRP to handle access to resources and it gives outstanding guarantees to race and deadlock-free preemptive execution and bounded priority inversion. Additionally, the model does not use excessive memory for the stack since the tasks all share common stack space. The predictable overhead combined with the aforementioned properties makes the framework amenable to static analysis.

The RTFM execution model imposes the following additional restriction to the more general SRP model: priorities must be static due to how tasks are mapped to hardware interrupt controller. For a system to be fully schedulable the deadline for sporadic tasks must be shorter than the inter-arrival time of the task, but this does not break the model since RTFM scheduling is "best effort".

RTFM implements best effort scheduling based on static task priorities. For static analysis under Rate Monotonic[3] scheduling, minimum inter-arrival is assumed to be larger or equal to the deadline of the task. If hard real-time guarantees are not required the model can be relaxed and allow for tasks over-running their deadlines. Notice however that hardware tasks are directly bound to interrupts which holds only a single bit buffer indicating that the task is pending (has been requested for execution). This buffer coalesces multiple (unattended) requests. Whether this behavior is acceptable is of course application dependent. On the one hand, coalescing leads to an error if the correctness relies on the fact that each arrival is accounted for. On the other hand, coalescing is acceptable in cases where it suffices as an indication that the task should run (e.g., to dequeue some hardware buffered data). In addition to hardware bound tasks, RTFM provides means to express software tasks with user defined buffering capacity. For RTFM systems with software tasks, the schedulability analysis extends on SRP as requiring the proof that each message buffer suffice.

Locks are single-unit, meaning they can not be simultaneously locked by multiple tasks, thus only one concurrent lock of a resource is allowed.

Tasks must also be run to completion with the exception of the special `idle` job which act as an endless loop or a sleep instruction such as a `wfi`.

The priority of the task is then bound to the interrupt service routine (ISR) matching that priority, associating an ISR to each task.

RTFM models priority as zero being the lowest and increasing numbers are of higher priority, thus a mapping between the hardware implementation and the framework is needed since the ARM Nested Vector Interrupt Controller (NVIC) models the highest priority being 0 and increasing numbers decrease in priority.

The SRP model has been extensively studied and a thorough understanding of the model and the available analysis methods that can be applied has been developed in the computer science community since the publication by Baker 3 decades ago.

1.1.4 Real-Time For the Masses (RTFM)

Real-Time For the Masses is a framework developed by the Embedded Systems group[18] at Luleå University of Technology (LTU) for leveraging the interrupt controller to schedule tasks of different priority, while the risk of deadlock is mitigated thanks to all resource-accesses being handled by the Stack Resource Policy (SRP). Message passing between tasks and scheduling of future tasks is also supported, creating a strong package where the nondeterminism[4] of a threaded execution model is avoided. This also lends itself to static analysis methods.

The early days

Real-Time For the Masses has seen many iterations over the years. As the conceptual idea matured it often outgrew the tools at hand leading to new and extended variants of the framework. Different languages and implementations has emerged. This is an overview. For the in-depth details the reader is encouraged to study the cited research papers.

In the beginning it consisted of a set of ideas:
- Reactive programming (real-time)
- Familiar notion of tasks and resources
- Stack Resource Policy (SRP) [2]

The first iteration as presented in [1] used a C-code API. This together with script tools for generating XML system models which then later could be analyzed by the user to assign proper resource ceilings. It did not however prevent the user from violating the programming model.

Becoming a language

The second iteration[5] was a Domain Specific Language (DSL) which compiled to C-code ready to compile for the desired target. The preprocessor stage were able to compute the resource ceilings and thus alleviated the need for external scripting tools and XML models[5, p. 1].

This second iteration was called *RTFM-lang* which in turn consisted of *RTFM-core* and *RTFM-kernel*. RTFM-core is written in OCaml/Menhir[19] and act as a compiler for RTFM-lang.

While still keeping to initial concepts presented above, this new development approach made it much more ergonomic to use.

Additionally, an object-oriented (OO) fronted for *RTFM-core* was developed[6] for *RTFM-lang*.

The next step for the framework follows after a discussion about Rust and how it differs from other systems programming languages.

1.1.5 Rust

Strengths of Rust

Safe Rust guarantees
- applications to be free of mutable aliasing,
- execution will have defined behavior at all times.

This is achieved by putting restrictions on the use of mutable references and precludes dereferencing of **raw** pointers (outside the control of the compiler).

In this way Rust fundamentally breaks with the tradition of systems level languages (like C/C++), under which accesses to memory are totally unrestricted. Whereas the C/C++ programmer has to be utterly careful to avoid running into memory un-safety (buffer overflow, use after free, etc), the Rust programmer can fearlessly focus on the problem at hand ensured that nothing neither can nor will go wrong[20].

The named restrictions are checked by the compiler that either proves the desired property (most cases), or if it deems it out of reach for static analysis, injects run-time verification code upholding the guarantees at run-time. In effect, a Rust application either operates correctly (as intended), or explicitly panics. Hence, Rust offers a means to implement, safe, secure and reliable applications with properties ensured by construction (rather then mere testing by the skillful C/C++ programmer).

So where is the catch?

In **safe** Rust[21], you cannot implement any type of sharing of mutable data between execution contexts (e.g., a sharing data between threads[22] or tasks). Neither can you implement interaction with the underlying hardware (e.g., reading and writing memory mapped registers), nor can you interact with external code (e.g., external bindings to libraries or operating system).

To this end, Rust introduces the notion of explicitly marked **unsafe** code, which lets you do exactly two things, 1) dereferencing raw pointers and 2) calling external code (all other safety mechanism are still in effect).

Rust provides an advanced type system used to create abstractions like Mutex types and Hardware Register Blocks. While this code is internally **unsafe** (and vetted by the developer) the user can access the abstractions from **safe** Rust.

In this way, there is a clear separation between the *minimal* chunks of **unsafe** code and the *large* bulk of application code/libraries written in **safe** Rust.

Rust provides a rich standard library, relying on dynamic memory allocation provided by the host operating system. The standard library is built on a core library, that neither requires dynamic allocations nor any host operating system and can thus be built for and executed on bare metal targets.

A minimal executable for a bare metal target requires just a few instructions for initializing static variables (globals) and a panic handler - in total a matter of bytes making Rust a contender even for the smallest of devices. Rust leverages the LLVM compiler infrastructure for backend code generation, which out the box is a cross compiler supporting the ARM Cortex M range of targets among others (MIPS, RISC-V etc.).

In the case of Rust, code is guaranteed to be free of mutable aliasing enabling extremely aggressive optimization by the LLVM compiler. In fact, Rust can claim zero-cost[23] abstractions[24]. Here zero-cost does not necessarily mean zero overhead, rather that the overhead is minimal and comes with a predictable cost. This holds for the core library but not necessarily for the standard library as it relies on services provided by non-Rust code (e.g., allocations provided by the host).

What does Rust's safety guarantees really mean? It does not prevent the programmer from writing code that is incorrect (there may still be bugs). However, applications in **safe** Rust can and will neither run into undefined behavior nor cause memory unsafety. Rust as a language has no notion of out-of-memory (OOM), it is merely a side effect of an allocator running out of resources. The standard library

---

models allocations as infallible (and in case it actually fails, it has to internally re-side to a panic). Notice, from a memory safety perspective panicking is always safe, as the program comes to a stop nothing bad (in the sense of memory accesses) will ever happen. In the setting of a critical system (safety/mission critical) this may be seen as intolerable as the availability of the system is traded for the sake of ensuring memory safety.

To this end, Rust allows panics to be unwrapped and handled, but error recovery is in general a hard problem (think of it, allocations can in the general case stem from anywhere in the application and libraries used, how could you sensibly deal with that)? Alternatively, one can adopt a custom allocator, e.g. heapless[7] which is fallible by construction (allowing the user to directly face OOM upfront, thus allowing system availability to be maintained, even if the allocator runs out of resources.

Even after all of this, there still remains a major concern regarding Rust memory safety, namely stack overflow. As an example, assume a shared memory space between stack and heap, if either overlaps the other havoc is to be expected. Rust assumes stack allocations to be infallible, but unlike the OOM case discussed previously, there is no guard available. Thus on a bare metal system (without any support for memory protection) havoc may be around the corner.

To this end, development of tooling around LLVM[8] has been conducted, to give safe estimates to stack memory requirements of Rust applications running on bare metal Cortex M targets.

With the use of fallible allocators (such as heapless) and static (compile-time) analysis of stack usage, the claim can be made that Rust is capable to offer reliability, availability and memory safety.

Rust code organisation terms and concepts

If the reader already is familiar with core terminology found in the Rust ecosystem, you may skip this section. If this is not the case, here are some core concepts regarding Rust project organisation.

Library One ore more modules used by other binaries or libraries

Binary Similar to a library, but gets linked into an executable binary

Module Used to organise code and manage scoping. Also the smallest unit which can be broken into its own file.

Crate A compilation unit, either a library or an executable binary, which is a collection of modules

Package One or more crates, at most one library

Workspace Allows multiple libraries unlike packages

Keyword `pub` Indicates that the item is *Public*, meaning it is accessible from outside of the modules own scope.

`crate::this::is::a::path` How paths to objects are written in Rust

Keyword `crate` This is the *root* of the crate, essentially the start of the path.

Keyword `super` This is used to refer to the parent scope of the path. Alleviates the need for hardcoding paths

Keyword self This is used to refer to the modules own scope.

For more detailed information chapter 7[25] of the Rust book is excellent. Another good resource is Rust by example[26] which also gives some more details about super and self[27].

Rust release channels

Nightly Bleeding edge development, no stability guarantees

Beta Every six weeks a **nightly** is promoted to **beta**, feature freeze

Stable Another six weeks and the bugfixed **beta** becomes **stable**

For more details see rustup documentation[28].

RTFM in Rust: The Next Generation

In 2017 Luleå University of Technology (LTU) opted to further investigate the opportunities to static memory safety offered by the recently released Rust language, and offered a granted Master thesis on the subject. The benefits of Rust as a programming language is thoroughly detailed in Chapter 3 of Jorge Aparicio's[29] Master thesis[9].

Jorge's thesis describes version v0.5.0 of the framework, and the multi-core extensions built into this release. The structural changes of the Rust port of the framework has seen some notable changes, described in the next section.

Evolution of Rust Real-Time For the Masses structure

The current day Real-Time For the Masses framework is a combination of three crates, `cortex-m-rtfm`, `rtfm-syntax` and `rtfm-core`. In the early days it started out as one singular library.

By version v0.2.0 of the framework the structure changed considerably when syntax parsing was separated into its own crate, `rtfm-syntax` and the majority of `cortex-m-rtfm` was restructured into a local nested crate named `macros`.

Version v0.3.0 remained largely the same code structure-wise, but in v0.4.0 a big transformation occurred. The part of the code doing the code generation was separated into its own module, the codebase almost doubled and the `macros`-crate became a workspace member. Additionally, the `rtfm-syntax` crate was inlined into the macro crate.

With the introduction of multi-core support, the structure was approaching the current day structure, where release v0.5.0 separated syntax parsing once more into a `rtfm-syntax` crate.

With the help of cargo-modules[30] it is possible to visualise the layout of modules and their visibility within simpler crates. Unfortunately, the tool is not yet compatible with features such as workspaces which is used in `cortex-m-rtfm`.

The legend for the colours of the graph, copied from `cargo-modules` documentation:

- Green nodes are public modules.
- Yellow nodes are private modules.
- Black nodes are external types or modules.
- Dotted nodes are conditional (test modules for example).
- Black edges denote a "is sub-module of" relation.
- Yellow/Green edges denote a 'use something of module' relation

The overview of the `rtfm-syntax` crate generated by the command seen in Listing 1.1.

```
cd rtic-syntax
git checkout v0.4.0
rustup run nightly cargo modules --orphans --enable-edition-2018 graph\
  --external --conditional --types > structure.dot
```

Listing 1.1: cargo `modules` generate module overview

After adding some styling to the dotfile, the result is found in Figure 1.1.

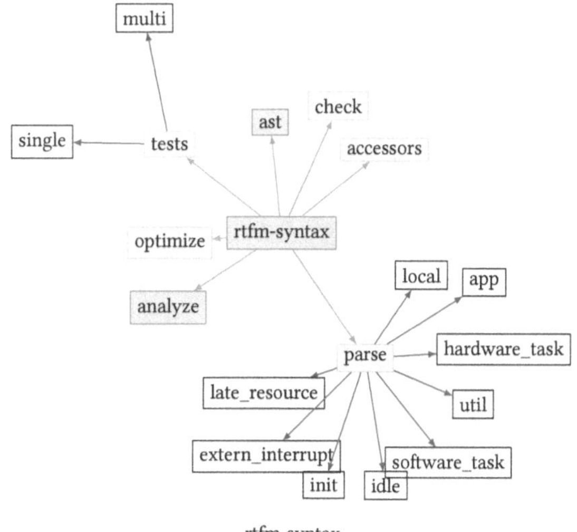

Figure 1.1: Structural layout of rtfm-syntax `v0.4.0`

1.1.6 RTFM becomes RTIC

There was more than one occasion where people in the community expressed discontent with the Real-Time For the Masses acronym "RTFM". Albeit well defined

Figure 1.2: RTIC Framework logo

what the intended meaning of the acronym is, it collides with another well-known acronym, especially within the realm of software development.

Thus, if searching the web for Real-Time For the Masses by the acronym the complete Internet archive of somewhat rude suggestions to study the manual also shows up.

With this in mind, there were attempts to change the name. The first round[31] trying to find a more suitable name saw many creative suggestions, but none that really caught on. It was decided that version v0.5.0 would be released under the original name. The second round, championed by James Munns in RFC 33[32] met more success.

The previously submitted name proposals were revisited and many new ones were proposed. Finally, a clear winner emerged, having qualities both as a full name and acronym. Additionally, it is partially identical to the old name, meaning the "brand" created by RTFM is not all lost while the search engine optimisation (SEO) for the project got improved.

The new name was voted through, implemented and the project is henceforth known as *Real-Time Interrupt-driven Concurrency*, or as the acronym *RTIC*.

The new name better relates to the functionality of the framework, since the primary focus is to provide a framework facilitating the development of *Real-Time* systems, since the primary means of interacting with the surroundings for such a system is via *interrupts*, while providing a concept of tasks that can run *concurrently* (taking turns).

The old name had troubles related to graphical branding, mainly because there were no clear concept to draw from the name itself. When pronouncing *RTIC* as a word, it sounds like the English word *arctic*, which is apt considering the origin of the framework itself and the graphical profile of LTU[33]. The new name was easier to conceptualise, and the logo is now a drawn picture of an Arctic fox, as seen in Figure 1.2.

This change of project name happened during the work of this thesis, and what was originally RTFM is now RTIC. Thus henceforth the new name will be used, but when referring to the older implementation the older name is used.

1.2 Motivation

With more and more embedded systems being deployed in areas ranging from common household items to mission-critical components of vehicles and industry the tools enabling the development of such systems becomes more important. With the trend seemingly only accelerating, the correctness and functionality of the systems also becomes more important as more of society relies on them, notable areas like communication and transportation relies heavily on this kind of technology.

When the complexity of the tasks the embedded systems are to perform demand some form of concurrency, many turn to Real-Time Operating Systems (RTOS), such as ChibiOS/RT, Contiki, FreeRTOS, QNX, Tock and VxWorks to name a few.

These RTOSes listed all employ a thread based execution model, which by design is hard to prove correct[4], there is the risk of deadlock when there are no strict policy such as Stack Resource Policy (SRP) enforcing how resources can be accessed in a safe manner.

Thus an easy to use and approachable non-thread based solution is lacking in the market. This is where Real-Time Interrupt-driven Concurrency (RTIC) stands out, it provides the common task abstractions developers are used to, with tasks, configurable priority levels, message passing between tasks and the ability to schedule tasks for the future with the guarantees of deadlock-free execution thanks to SRP.

Rust is a relatively young language with strong beneficial features in regards to memory safety; using a strong static type system together with a borrow-checker which moves whole categories of errors to compile time rather than run-time. With a fast pace of development, strong community driven open-source mentality and good likeability[34] Rust provides a compelling alternative to other programming languages and ecosystems.

As the Rust language is improved and the feature-set extended, it is possible to achieve cleaner and more idiomatic[35] implementations of things previously requiring workarounds due to language limitations. For each new release[36] of the stable Rust compiler, which happens every 6 weeks, improvements are made across the whole ecosystem relying on Rust.

Combining these, the memory safety guarantees from Rust, together with the deadlock-free properties of SRP and the usability properties including the familiar notion of tasks provided by RTIC the future of embedded systems development can be improved.

This is an attempt to improve the experience with RTIC, both for developers and end-users by updating it to the latest available tooling and implementing long-standing feature-requests while investigating if the current structure and design can be further improved to enable and encourage extensions rather than requiring special use-cases to diverge by creating a fork of the framework. Thereby creating a stronger incentive for commercial interests to build upon the foundation provided by RTIC while making it easy and attractive to contribute back to RTIC, improving the framework for all users. The sustainability of the project lies in the hands of both developers and users, something commonly found in open-source projects.

1.3   Problem Definition

Looking back at the original name, *Real-Time For the Masses*, the idea is that it should be approachable for novices as well as powerful enough for more seasoned embedded developers. The RTIC framework has yet to reach this goal, there is always room for improvement may it be ergonomics, feature-set, support tooling or how it is taught via documentation or examples.

1.3.1 Overview: Pain points

A list of general pain points of RTFM v0.5[37] which needed addressing:
- Usability and consistency
  - Fear of Rust Macros
  - Non-idiomatic workarounds
- Code structure - reuse and modularity
- Implementation complexity
- CI testing and tools

1.3.2 Detailed descriptions

Usability and consistency

The RTIC framework expects the user to write code which the Rust attribute macro can parse. Due to past limitations of the Rust language sometimes workarounds had to be implemented to achieve the desired functionality.

Sometimes this resulted in less than stellar user interfaces (UI), where there were different ways to annotate somewhat similar functionality.

Issues to deal with:
- Asymmetric UI for specifying resources, tasks, idle and init
- Asymmetric UI for locking resources[38]
- Not possible to abstract away locking for resources known to be lock-free or only accessed by one task[39]
- Asymmetry in #[init] in regard to `LateResources`
- Unusual construct for specifying interrupts used to dispatch software tasks
- Provide the special `CriticalSection` token some Hardware Abstraction Layers (HAL) require

The benefits of a symmetric user interface are that if you want to change one smaller detail this does not force a cascade of dependent changes due to the different requirements related to the small change. It is not always achievable with full symmetry, but above is a listing of the asymmetric pain points frequently questioned by members of the RTIC community. These are overrepresented among the questions from beginners and seasoned embedded developers alike.

Beginning with the first in the list above, the way to specify/annotate which behaviour a function is to perform. Each of `task`, `idle` and `init` are applied as an attribute on the Rust function itself, including the way how to specify a default value for *early resources*. The way to specify the resource struct is by knowing that the struct must be named `Resources`.

This could be an attribute like the other, then the case-sensitivity and specific name of the struct would not be important.

See Listing 1.2 for a reference on the syntax for #[task], #[init], #[init(0)], #[idle] and struct Resources.

```rust
 1    struct Resources {
 2        // A resource
 3        #[init(0)]
 4        shared: u32,
 5    }
 6
 7    #[init]
 8    fn init(_: init::Context) -> init::LateResources {
 9        init::LateResources {}
10    }
11
12    #[idle]
13    fn idle(_cx: idle::Context) -> ! {
14    }
15
16    #[task(binds = UART0, resources = [shared])]
17    fn uart0(mut cx: uart0::Context) {
18    }
```

Listing 1.2: Collection of examples of asymmetry

Second in the list which is one of the trickier problems people unfamiliar with the framework experience is that it is possible to get errors looking like Listing 1.3 after changing the priority of a task previously lower in priority to highest in priority. The asymmetric lock UI requires the user to change where the locks are taken. The user must change all the previous higher prio tasks to take the lock, and remove the lock from the new highest task.

The solution is to change the UI to always require taking the lock, but to optimise it away when not needed. The LLVM compiler can infer which task is the highest priority during compilation and the code for locking the resource can be optimised away, while all other tasks remain as they were. This would remove the need of moving where locks are taken and thus the experience would be more seamless.

The third item in the list are related to the previous, some resources can optionally be exempt from the need to lock them. Instead of having to always use the lock for these special resources they could be annotated within the resources struct and then during compilation verified that they adhere to the locking properties requested by the user.

The proposed locking properties are `#[lock_free]` and `#[task_local]`. If a resource is shared by tasks with the same priority a resource can be `#[lock_free]` since the tasks never will preempt another task at the same priority. `#[task_local]` means that the resource becomes exclusive to one singular task.

The fourth item is also resource related, but this time the problem is if a *late resource*[40] is introduced the function signature and return value must change for the `#[init]` function. The same goes if removing the last *late resource*.

The fifth issue is related to the non-idiomatic way to specify which interrupt handler shall deal with software tasks.

The final issue is a convenience feature for people required to use some specific HAL requiring a unique `bare_metal::CriticalSection` which has the special property that it cannot be created by the user. By providing a default `CriticalSection` as part of the RTIC task Context for init it should be available to any user needing it.

```
$ git checkout v0.5.1

$ sd "binds = GPIOA" "binds = GPIOA, priority = 3" examples/lock.rs

$ cargo check --example lock
    Checking cortex-m-rtfm v0.5.1
error[E0599]: no method named `lock` found for mutable reference `&mut u32`
 in the current scope
  --> examples/lock.rs:30:28
   |
30 |            c.resources.shared.lock(|shared| {
   |                               ^^^^ method not found in `&mut u32`
   |
   = note: the method `lock` exists but the following trait bounds were not
   satisfied:
            `u32: rtfm::Mutex`
            which is required by `&mut u32: rtfm::Mutex`

error[E0614]: type `resources::shared<'_>` cannot be dereferenced
  --> examples/lock.rs:53:9
   |
53 |          *c.resources.shared += 1;
   |          ^^^^^^^^^^^^^^^^^^^^

error[E0614]: type `resources::shared<'_>` cannot be dereferenced
  --> examples/lock.rs:55:38
   |
55 |          hprintln!("D - shared = {}", *c.resources.shared).unwrap();
   |                                       ^^^^^^^^^^^^^^^^^^^^

error: aborting due to 3 previous errors
< cut>
```

Listing 1.3: By raising the priority of a task above the previous highest priority task also using that resource, the requirement of locking moves causing these errors.

Macros

Code generation is done via Rust macros[41] detailed in the *advanced features* part of the Rust book. Macros are what is known as *metaprogramming*, which essentially is writing code which manipulates code. As described in the book referenced above:

> The downside to implementing a macro instead of a function is that macro definitions are more complex than function definitions because you're writing Rust code that writes Rust code. Due to this indirection, macro definitions are generally more difficult to read, understand, and maintain than function definitions.

The tooling for debugging rust macros are not easy to use, even though tools like cargo-expand[42] significantly improves the situation. It produces the *expanded* output of the macro, meaning that the code passed to the compiler can be inspected in order to verify correct operation.

Another way to debug Rust macros is to use the rather cumbersome `external-macro-backtrace`[43] tool only available on the **nightly** channel.

Since the general complexity of Rust macros is higher than *regular* Rust code due to the indirection described above, many find it a daunting task to get a good understanding of the framework's inner workings.

Workarounds

As the Rust language mature language limitations gets resolved, and previous "scary-looking" workarounds for things previously not supported can be removed. Thus usability can be improved.

A notable workaround in the case of RTFM was where to place the app-macro acting as the starting point of the framework. Without support for an attribute on a proper Rust module a constant was used instead since `const`s had support for attributes. Proper support for attributes on modules landed in Rust version 1.42.0 implemented in pull request 64273[44]. Listing 1.4 gives an example of the syntax difference. The syntax is not the only change, proper modules require that all the semantics follow regular Rust module semantics.

```
1   // Constant acting as a module
2   #[attribute]
3   const APP: () = {...};
4
5   // Proper Rust module
6   #[attribute]
7   mod name_of_mod {...}
```

Listing 1.4: The Rust const item instead of mod workaround

Code structure

RTIC is already divided into multiple crates, see rtic-rs[45] organisation on GitHub and crates.io[46] for sources.

cortex-m-rtic Wrapper and outermost crate, tests, examples

cortex-m-rtic-macros Contains the macro and code generation

rtic-syntax Validating input syntax and performing analysis

rtic-core Some core abstractions common for RTIC

In addition to these crates, the codebase is divided into multiple modules and while the structure is clearly thought through, the overall complexity discourages potential contributors whom do not have the time to invest into studying it thoroughly.

The current layout of the project is not designed with extensibility in mind, this has not been a requirement. However, it is designed to be easy to create ports for other hardware platforms, where `rtic-core` and `rtic-syntax` are common between ports, but code generation and hardware related logic is contained within `cortex-m-rtic` for the ARM `Cortex-M` version. The need for structural changes to allow extensions stems from the fact that Rust's package manager cargo does not permit code changes/replacement during compilation.

The current option is to create a copy of the code (fork) and modify it, with an overwhelming risk that future improvements of the original project never gets back-ported and that the chances of getting the extension back upstream gets slimmer for each update of each separate code base. Diverging common-ancestor open-source projects are not unheard of, for good or for worse.

It can lead to duplication of efforts hindering the overall innovation ability, or on the other hand it also can bring new ideas and energy into a stale project.

If the code could be structured in such a way that it would be *minimal* overall impact to change select parts of the implementation, then the risk would be substantially reduced since getting the updated core parts would not conflict with the code of the extensions. Granted, the extensions may need to be updated for breaking API changes, but that is much more feasible.

Such structure would allow commercial interests to develop extensions to satisfy their domain specific needs, examples could be static code analysis, including Worst-Case Execution Time (WCET), task response time and overall schedulability analysis, or generating some specific output for external tools.

Complexity

Full understanding of the code generation is not imperative for using the framework, it can be used as a "black box", but if things go wrong and the documentation does not specify how things are done, many developers turn directly to the code for understanding the implementation details. As discussed previously understanding and then debugging Rust macros is one major roadblock many get dissuaded by due to the general complexity.

Another drawback related to the complexity is that building extensions or modifying the source to reach the desired behaviour is not easy, hindering the community uptake and development of prototypes for new functionality.

CI testing and tools

The quality and functionality of the tools available makes a huge difference for both developers and end-users, with an experience ranging from fighting to even get the smallest thing going or to breeze through complex changes with confidence and ease.

It is important that the Version Control System (VCS) and hosting platform supports collaborative editing, allows for sensible code review and feedback.

Not only that, users considering contributing to the project should find the support structures in place helpful and encouraging. Such structures can be documentation how issues and bugs best are reported, or how to add feature requests.

In the case of RTIC, development is conducted at GitHub rtic-rs[47] where the organization *RTIC-rs* maintains all the repositories directly related to RTIC.

The tests for the code is automated and done on every Pull Request (PR) and also on every merge to the master branch. For a primer on Git and branching, see the Git book[48].

Such automation of testing is an important part of *Continuous Integration* (CI). If the test suite takes too long to complete there becomes a pause of uncertainty where the developer either has to context-switch completely and work on some other task, or just idle while the tests are performed, waiting for the tests to indicate success or failure of the current implementation. This break of cadence can be quite a time-sink. Tests should ideally fail as early as possible during the test run, if they fail at all, to reduce overall time spent waiting on test results.

The test setup in use is the open-source Continuous Integration platform Travis CI[49].

The time for a complete test cycle is roughly 15 minutes with Travis CI.

When a PR is submitted, the test suite runs and indicates whether it is permissible to merge or not. If permissible, the reviewer has to approve or request further changes. In case modifications are needed, another run of the tests is done. If no changes are needed and the reviewer approves the PR, then Bors[50] the merge bot begins by testing the merge of the PR to a staging branch. If this is successful, the proper merge against master follows.

Thus, for a successful merge against master at least two successful runs of the test suite are required, and that is if the reviewer ignores the initial PR test outcome. This sometimes happens when the changes in the PR only affects documentation or other things where the tests are unable to actually test the changes.

A typical scenario may look as follows: A developer submit a PR, one test is run. The reviewer find something odd, and requests changes. Changes are implemented and the tests are automatically re-run. Since the reviewer is happy, the PR gets approved and the `bors merge` command is issued telling the Bors merge bot to start the actual merge.

Bors starts the test for the `staging` branch which passes, then another test is run when the changes are in master. The PR is now fully merged. In total 4 passes with the test suite to get this change implemented.

With four passes each 15 minutes, that becomes one hour, and if both the developer and reviewer "babysit" the tests a worst case of two hours "wasted".

If cutting the test time by a factor 5 down to 3 minutes, that total time shrinks to a more manageable 24 minutes for the same worst case detailed above. In terms of *wall clock* time the whole change could be done in 12 minutes plus human overhead.

1.4   Delimitations

The original plan was to fully implement the proposed structural changes, as seen in section 3.4, but it quickly became apparent that to achieve the changes required for such a massive structural modification the proper channels through the open-source

RTIC community had to be used. Especially since the goal was to reduce the creation of hard to merge forks, it did not seem wise to do what you try to avoid.

Thus, the best way to drive change within the community is to join and become part of the project itself.

By becoming a core developer a new set of responsibilities not accounted for in the original plan made the full implementation fall outside the scope of this thesis.

Other areas briefly touched upon which also are outside the scope of this work includes formal verification and Async/await.

1.5 Contributions of this thesis

This thesis aims to improve the current state of the Rust embedded systems concurrency framework known as Real-Time Interrupt-driven Concurrency (RTIC), the outset was to improve the internal structure to improve extensibility. By doing this, the ability to build extensions could encourage all users, from hobbyists to professionals, to tailor it to their specific needs without having to create a fork of the project and cause divergence within the community. The theoretical design work how to approach this task is part of the thesis.

The main contribution are improvements of the RTIC framework itself, ranging from large structural changes in order to simplify the codebase to improved usability, documentation and teaching materials.

This thesis also deals with how the tools, primarily the Continuous Integration suites, surrounding state of the art software development can be leveraged to maximise productivity while ensuring correctness of the software being developed.

Furthermore, the role of being a core developer of the RTIC framework, a part of the Rust embedded community, as well as the Rust community in general, is discussed.

1.6 Outline

This thesis is structured as follows.

1.6.1 Chapter 1

Section 1.1 gives a background to the world of open-source software development and the licensing policies commonly used. It briefly describes Stack Resource Policy (SRP) and aims to explain core concepts found in the Rust ecosystem as well as the concept of Rust's memory guarantees. Then a description of the evolution of RTFM and the structural composition of the software in retrospect.

Section 1.2 motivates why this work is needed by showing where RTIC fills a place in the embedded systems market.

Section 1.3 outlines the limitations of the current RTIC implementation described as pain points for users interacting with the framework.

Section 1.4 discusses the delimitations and scope of the work.

Section 1.5 summarises the contributions made by this thesis.

1.6.2 Chapter 2

Section 2.1 provides an overview of common methods how to structure Rust projects by looking at different examples and discussing the support tools available. Section 2.2 discusses a few of the existing Real-time Operating Systems (RTOS) and compare them to RTIC. Section 2.3 introduces the premier resource for embedded development on Rust, the Rust Embedded Work Group.

1.6.3   Chapter 3

In section 3.1 the Rust way to handle packages and resources are detailed, followed by section 3.2 how RTIC Framework deals with resources and tasks. Section 3.3 details the "before" image of the RTIC framework, before any structural changes were made. Section 3.4 proposes ways to improve the current structural layout of RTIC while section 3.5 discusses Continuous Integration tools.

1.6.4   Chapter 4

Implementation notes about
- Modules instead of Const (section 4.1)
- Improvements of the CI tests (section 4.2)
- Renaming RTFM to RTIC (section 4.3)
- The removal of multi-core support (section 4.4)
- Structural layout changes of RTIC (section 4.5)

1.6.5   Chapter 5

This chapter aims to evaluate and present the results of framework improvements
- How work is screened by means of continuous peer-review to ensure high quality implementations (section 5.1)
- The results of using modules instead of const items (section 5.2)
- Evaluates the change of CI suite (section 5.3)
- Sums up the project name change and its impact (section 5.4)
- The impact on the project complexity after the removal of multi-core support (section 5.5)
- Changes to project structure (section 5.6)

1.6.6   Chapter 6

Section 6.1 discusses the role of a core developer of an open-source project within the embedded Rust community followed by a discussion on dealing with the identified pain points and their solutions.
- Usability and consistency and the impact of complex macros and workarounds (section 6.2)
- Code structure - modularity and complexity (section 6.3)
- Continuous Integration (section 6.4)

1.6.7   Chapter 7

Sums up the work and outlines future work within the field.

Chapter 2

Related work

This chapter presents the flexibility of the Rust way to structure source code by study-ing two different approaches.

Furthermore, a look into the common real-time operating systems and how they differ to the RTIC framework.

2.1 Structuring Rust projects

Structuring larger source code projects for modularity is dependent on the project itself, the tools at hand and the desired level of modularity.

The flexibility of Rust allows for different kinds of structures, each project have different needs and developers have preferences, thus there is no "one size fits all" recipe to adhere to. Rust provides Clippy[1] which is a collection of lints for Rust code with the intent to improve clarity and correctness by warning about known anti-patterns in Rust.

2.1.1 Clippy

Not to be confused with Microsoft Office Clippit, often nicknamed **Clippy**, as seen in Figure 2.1 together with Ferris the unofficial Rust mascot[2]. Artwork found here[3] in a post by Axel Navarro. Clippit surely did inspire the name of Rust Clippy and their nagging abilities are common strengths.

Since Rust is a moving target, having Clippy as a reference to what is considered "well written" Rust is g reat. However, for some projects some of the lints are not beneficial and overly restricting, which Clippy handles by letting you as developer configure what lints to enforce based on what you consider "acceptable style".

2.1.2 Flat hierarchical projects

An example of Rust flexibility, in the project just[4] which is a Make-inspired com-mand runner written in Rust the author prefers[5] a flat module tree in contrast to

Figure 2.1: Unofficial Rust mascot Ferris and Microsoft Clippy

nested module structure often seen[6] in Rust projects.

The author uses a fuzzy file searcher to navigate the code base, so the 80 or so source files all placed in `src/` becomes manageable.

2.1.3   Nested hierarchical projects

As an example of a more "traditional" nested layout, the developers over at Datalust.co shares how they decided to structure their software `flair`[7].

Another strength of Rust is the ability to adapt the project structure along the way, reducing the risk of getting stuck in mess. The author "Ghost" provides a step-by-step project structure transformation guide in a post[8], making a great example of the information provided in the Rust book. These steps show how code structure can be modified to adopt to a growing codebase.

The most downloaded crate on crates.io, rand[9], which is built by the Rand Project and the Rust Project developers presents a typical Rust crate layout with multiple crates wrapped into a workspace. This enables convenient testing for each crate but does not limit for example benchmarks to access the whole workspace. See Listing 2.1 for how the `workspace` members are declared in Cargo.toml[10].

```
[workspace]
members = [
    "rand_core",
    "rand_distr",
    "rand_chacha",
    "rand_hc",
    "rand_pcg",
]
```

Listing 2.1: Workspace members in rand

The modules of rand_core can be studied in Figure 2.2.

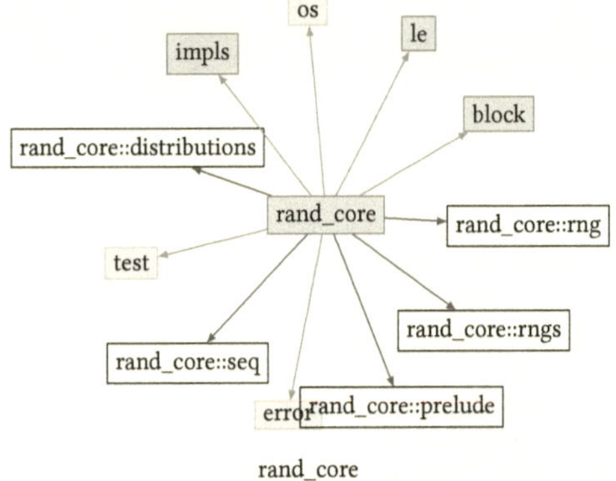

Figure 2.2: Modules of the rand_core crate

2.2 Real-Time Operating Systems

Notes about the available Real-Time Operating Systems (RTOS) alternatives.

Many of these alternatives are not suitable to run on small and resource constrained hardware commonly found in embedded systems. There are applications where embedded systems need more capabilities, such as the display unit in a modern vehicle dealing both with navigation, multimedia and high-resolution screens with touch-interfaces. Larger embedded devices includes processors featuring multiple cores, relatively massive amounts of RAM (several gigabytes) and ample storage space.

Such hardware is now readily available for consumers too thanks to projects like Raspberry Pi[11] and the many clones following the success of that project. The Raspberry Pi primarily runs a full-fledged Linux based environment, but Windows IoT and different flavours of BSD are also supported. In addition to the common operating systems, these devices allow development of experimental operating systems, self-study material[12] and research-projects accessible for a wider user-base.

2.2.1 RTOS

- Threaded
    - Chibios[13]
    - Contiki[14] (protothreads = "stackless threads")
    - FreeRTOS[15]
    - QNX[16]
    - Tock[17] (Written in Rust!)
    - VxWorks[18]
- Async/await and optional threads
    - Drone OS[19] (Also Rust, async/await and optional multi-stack threads)

These all have different strengths and weaknesses, but in contrast to the RTIC framework they all are primarily thread based except Drone OS. Threads can be made to work and these projects are examples of that. The correctness lies with the developer since the model by itself is prone to non-determinism caused by the threaded execution model.

Drone OS and Tock stands out since they are written in Rust and thus has more in common with RTIC in regards to the memory safety properties Rust provides.

In their book[20] describing the operating system their design principles are as follows, quoted:

- Energy effective from the start. Drone encourages interrupt-driven execution model.
- Hard Real-Time. Drone relies on atomic operations instead of using critical sections.
- Fully preemptive multi-tasking with strict priorities. A higher priority task takes precedence with minimal latency.
- Highly concurrent. Multi-tasking in Drone is very cheap, and Rust ensures it is also safe.
- Message passing concurrency. Drone ships with synchronization primitives out of the box.
- Single stack by default. Drone concurrency primitives are essentially stackless state machines. But stackful tasks are still supported.
- Dynamic memory enabled. Drone lets you use convenient data structures like mutable strings or vectors while still staying deterministic and code efficient.

Drone OS by default relies on Rust async/await features, their documentation[21] has nice illustrations of concurrently running tasks. Drone OS relies on the Nested Vector Interrupt Controller (NVIC) to do priority based preemption, and the single stack is managed by Rust's async/await where tasks are run to completion. The commonalities with RTIC becomes apparent except for the difference in scheduling and resource management.

The most rigorously tested operating system microkernel available is called seL4[22] and the testing is not only dynamic testing, but seL4 is formally proven to be correct, which is a much stronger claim than "we did not find problems during testing"-correct.

Hardware support[23] for seL4 is primarily larger systems, from x86 to ARMv7A, ARMv8A and RISC-V. seL4 is not intended to be run on smaller resource constrained embedded systems.

2.2.2   Async/await, the Future is .await()ed

Can be implemented both with and without threads as noted by Jorge in a blog post[24] detailing the current state of async/await on embedded Rust. The concept with async/await is to not block but rather return a Future which then can be used to enable asynchronous multitasking[25] without using threads.

There are some caveats when considering to implement multitasking with async/await, namely the returned Future must be run to completion. This is the same requirement tasks in RTIC has and there is ongoing work implementing support for async/await for RTIC[26].

2.3   Embedded systems leveraging Rust

The Rust Embedded devices Working Group[27] is an effort "towards making Rust a great choice for embedded development"[28].

The Rust-embedded book[29] and the bookshelf[30] are resources provided to make the learning experience of Rust and Embedded as good as possible. Another good resource is the awesome-embedded-rust[31] list of awesome projects and tools. Having such a comprehensive index of Hardware Abstraction Layers (HAL), Board Support Crates (BSP) and drivers is truly "amazing".

Under the heading "Real-time"[32] the available projects are grouped if they are a real-time Operating System or a real-time tool.

The RTOSes listed are Drone OS[33], discussed in the previous section, two different[34] interfaces[35] to FreeRTOS and Tock[36].

RTIC is the sole member of the real-time tool group in this list.

Chapter 3 Theory

This chapter aims to describe the technical underpinnings of the tools at hand.

3.1   The Rust package system
Rust comes with its own preferred package manager, cargo.

3.1.1   Package manager: cargo
Cargo is the preferred tool to manage dependencies and dependency resolution in the Rust ecosystem. Similarly like many other programming languages has their own package manager. For example, Python has pip, Java has Maven (not limited to Java), JavaScript uses npm and Ruby has RubyGems. The larger a software project is, the amount of external dependencies tend to grow, and with this growth the complexity of resolving the dependency graph in- creases. The different package managers have different approaches to the problem, and it has been shown1 by Russ Cox that the problem itself is NP-Complete2.
Rust's cargo dependency resolution counters this problem not with the help of "SAT solvers" like some other package managers, but by changing some of the as- sumptions Russ used when creating the proof:

1 A package can list zero or more packages or specific package versions as depen- dencies.
2 To install a package, all its dependencies must be installed.
3 Each version of a package can have different dependencies.
4 Two different versions of a package cannot be installed simultaneously.

Cargo's method is to relax both number 1 and number 4, that is, cargo allows the author to use permissible ranges of versions with the help of Semantic Versioning (semver)3 in conjunction with allowing duplication of dependencies. The amount of duplication is reduced thanks to the use of semantic versioning. It could be considered a hybrid approach[4].

Thus cargo can use a less complex backtracking solver rather than a SAT solver. As this is not a perfect solution to the dependency problem, it goes a long way in solving the majority of common dependency situations[5].

Additionally, cargo provides a convenient interface to most tasks related to software development, creating new projects, syntax checking, compiling the software, running tests, interfacing with the documentation, adding dependencies and publishing the result to the Rust community's crate registry crates.io[6].

3.1.2 Rust project levels of abstraction

The multiple layers of abstraction available in the Rust language allows for almost any use-case.

Here is an overview:

Module

The second smallest unit of privacy are the modules, which are the smallest unit which can be broken into its own file. Comparable to C-files or Java classes. The file system can act together with Rust modules to create nice structural grouping of source code.

Something which differ from other languages is that the file system is not automatically parsed, Rust requires the developer to explicitly define which modules are to be included, and that is not in the file itself, but from the file or module which will use it.

Additionally, modules are the premier means of scoping and privacy. To control scoping and privacy, the keyword pub is added to items to allow access from outside the module scope. By default all items has private visibility.

Thus Rust makes the developer think through each action, the module tree is not automatically built, visibility is not automatically inferred. Fine-grained control is achieved through explicit annotation.

Crate

The crate is a compilation unit producing either a library or multiple executable binaries, often including and combining external dependencies into the build.

Package

A set of crates, which could consist of one single crate, that belongs together to provide the desired functionality.

Workspace

A composition of crates, allowing cargo to act on multiple crates as if they were one.

3.1.3 Typical structural evolution of a software project

As a project evolves the need for restructuring usually arises for some reason or another.

Design driven development may have made some incorrect assumptions or during implementation realised better methods to achieve the desired goals, for implementation based it could be that the initial prototype has grown enough to require looking over splitting into libraries or just modules (files).

3.2 RTIC Resources and Tasks

The Real-Time Interrupt-driven Concurrency framework needs a well-defined way to reason about the units of work it will perform, called tasks, and the resources to work upon.

3.2.1 Embedded systems in general

An embedded system is a system embedded within a larger system, performing some specific function of that system. The hardware requirements varies in relation to the complexity of that specific function, from the smallest microcontroller to impressive multi-core setups.

The system typically can be modeled as a "black box", see Figure 3.1 which has a set of inputs, and a set of outputs. From the view of the whole system the internals of the embedded system are not important, what matters is that the desired output is produced for a defined input.

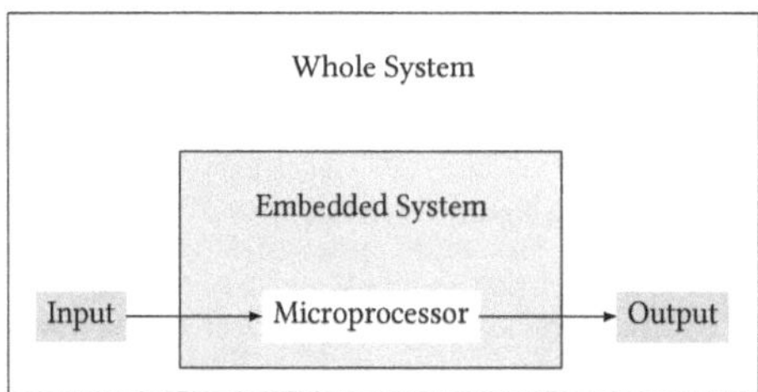

Figure 3.1: Black-box model of an embedded system

Additionally, this output may have a requirement about the permissible time frame the output is still relevant, meaning it has a deadline. Systems where meeting the deadline is a requirement and often even imperative for the functionality of the system are referred to as *real-time* systems. Another term for a real-time system is that it follows *reactive computing* paradigms.

The importance of the real-time property can also be specified, where a *hard real-time* system is a system where a missed deadline means total system failure. There also exists "softer" real-time systems where a missed deadline is not fatal. An example of a hard real-time system, the Anti-lock Braking System (ABS) of a car must act within its deadline, else the purpose and benefit of ABS is negated. There exists systems where "hard" and "soft" real-time components coexist. Typically done as a separation of critical and non-critical tasks, where the non-critical task are done by a "best-effort" basis.

3.2.2 RTIC Task and Resource model

RTIC allows the user to define resources[7] which could be data structures, references to initialized peripherals or the references to peripherals themselves. These resources can be associated to tasks, which RTIC have two types of:

Hardware tasks Scheduled by hardware

Software tasks Scheduled by other tasks

Resources can be initialised directly, called *Early resources* or later on in the special function annotated with the #[init][8] attribute during runtime. Resources initialised during runtime within this init function are called "Late resources".

To prevent race conditions to resources RTIC utilises the well-proven Stack Resource Policy (SRP) [2]. The RTIC implementation of the SRP model imposes some further limitations on the more general SRP model discussed in section 1.1.3.

These limitations, namely:

- Single-unit resources
- Static priorities
- Sporadic task deadline must be less than the inter-arrival time for hardware tasks[9]
- Resources must be locked in a Last-In, First-Out (LIFO) manner

Software task[10] on the other hand can be queued by the task dispatcher and the size of the queue is controlled by the capacity argument to the task. This allows to send bursts of more task invocations than a hardware task could handle, but limited by the queue size. Thus RTIC is mixed critical if using software tasks, since it is possible to have potentially failing (unable to queue) soft real-time tasks at lower priority than the hard real-time tasks at higher priority.

Summarising, if the low priority task is unable to queue due to full queues, it is not fatal to the system and no memory safety violation will occur.

RTIC task may be given access to resources, accessed through a special *Context* provided by RTIC, details of this context can be studied in [9, p.27].

The interrupt controller of ARM is called *Nested Vector Interrupt Control* (NVIC)[11]. The purpose of NVIC is to prioritise input stimuli and execute functions defined for that stimuli, called Interrupt Service Routine (ISR). Then when the ISR has finished execution the program resumes where it were previously. Both hardware and software can generate interrupts.

RTIC works by reacting to the interrupts provided by NVIC, as instructed by the developer. Software tasks need a configured interrupt from the NVIC to be able to be scheduled.

This is one of the true strengths of RTIC as a system, since the NVIC handles scheduling both latency and overhead is minimal and the hardware provides for reliable operation.

Below in Figure 3.2 a schematic view of how RTIC, NVIC and the rest of the embedded system interface with its surroundings.

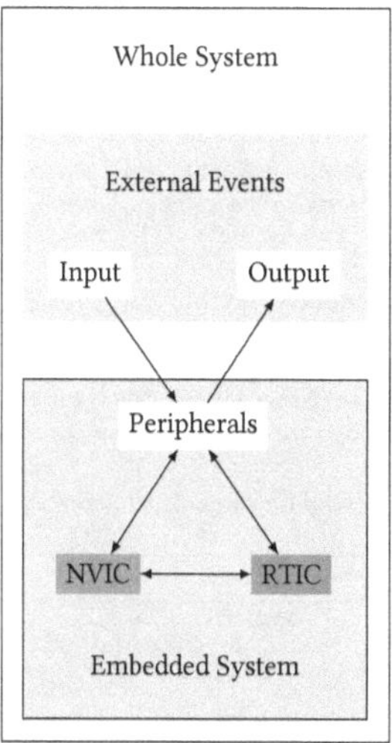

Figure 3.2: How RTIC typically interfaces with the surroundings

Thus tasks in RTIC are run directly by the ISRs of the NVIC. The *Nested* in Nested Vector Interrupt Control says that the interrupts may be configured to preempt each other. If two interrupts are of different priorities the higher priority interrupt may preempt the lower priority one, but not the other way around.

Another way to control which interrupts may get executed is by modifying the PRIMASK and BASEPRI registers of NVIC. BASEPRI is heavily used by RTIC since it directly correlates to the SRP concept of the system ceiling [2, s 3.2].

That is, the *dynamic priority* is used to ensure that during a critical section no *lower priority* task may interrupt by raising the BASEPRI. For more in-depth on the concepts of ceiling analysis and critical sections refer to the RTIC manual here[12] and here[13].

3.3   Current structural layout of RTIC

This section describes the current source code structure and the current limitations in regard to extensibility.

3.3.1 Dependencies

The tool `cargo-deps` as used in Figure 1.1 is currently unable to function properly for crates using the `workspaces` feature. Instead `cargo depgraph`[14] can be used to show all the dependencies, it however does not attempt to describe the internal code structure.

This is the command to only output the relation between the core dependencies of RTIC, there are a multitude of other build dependencies and libraries in use. However, trying to fit all of these into one graph is not feasible within the boundaries of a single page. If one would remove the `--focus names,...` argument the full graph would be presented.

```
cargo depgraph --focus cortex-m-rtfm,rtfm-syntax,rtfm-core > structure.dot
```

The following graph displays the current dependency structure of version `v0.5.1` of `cortex-m-rtfm` which was released before the beginning of this work. Thus version `v0.5.1` will be regarded as the baseline of comparison.

In Figure 3.3 the structure of the crate dependencies are outlined.

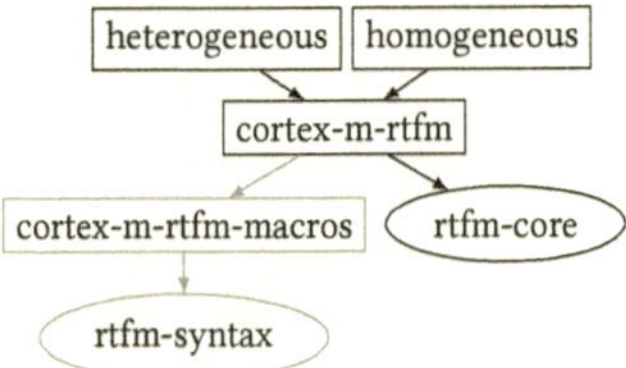

Figure 3.3: Structural layout of cortex-m-rtfm `v0.5.1`

The crates `heterogeneous` and `homogeneous` provides the multi-core support, described in [9, chapter 5], these are by default disabled and behind a cargo feature as well as requiring a nightly compiler.

These will be excluded from the structural analysis to simplify graphs and discussion.

3.3.2 Internal structure

Next an attempt at describing the modular structure within the macro crate.

The full modular structure of `cortex-m-rtfm-macros` can be studied in Listing 3.1. Each file only contains one module. In Rust it is possible to have multiple modules within a single file, even nested modules are supported, but since in this case each file represents their own module we can exploit regular system utilities to describe the structure.

As expected the majority of code is found within the module codegen since `rtfm-syntax` is responsible for both parsing and analysis. Then one may ask why there seems to be duplication of the `analysis` and `check` module, since these are also present in `rtfm-syntax` as seen in Listing 3.2.

```
$ tree macros/
macros/
├── Cargo.toml
└── src
    ├── analyze.rs
    ├── check.rs
    ├── codegen
    │   ├── assertions.rs
    │   ├── dispatchers.rs
    │   ├── hardware_tasks.rs
    │   ├── idle.rs
    │   ├── init.rs
    │   ├── locals.rs
    │   ├── module.rs
    │   ├── post_init.rs
    │   ├── pre_init.rs
    │   ├── resources.rs
    │   ├── resources_struct.rs
    │   ├── schedule_body.rs
    │   ├── schedule.rs
    │   ├── software_tasks.rs
    │   ├── spawn_body.rs
    │   ├── spawn.rs
    │   ├── timer_queue.rs
    │   └── util.rs
    ├── codegen.rs
    ├── lib.rs
    ├── tests
    │   ├── multi.rs
    │   └── single.rs
    └── tests.rs

3 directories, 26 files
```

Listing 3.1: Structure of `cortex-m-rtfm-macros`

The reason for this is to encourage simple and straightforward implementations
of other hardware architectures than ARM Cortex-M, as described by Rust port cre-
ator Jorge Aparicio in a blogpost[15] before the release of version `v0.5.x` of the framework.

In addition to this, in the same post under the header *Supporting other architectures*[16] an experimental port for regular `x86_64` Linux[17] platform is announced.

Other ports exists, one to the RISC-V microcontroller HiFive1[18] by David Craven
of the riscv-rust team, and one targeting the `msp430`[19] microcontroller. Iqclusion also

```
$ tree src/
src/
├── accessors.rs
├── analyze.rs
├── ast.rs
├── check.rs
├── lib.rs
├── optimize.rs
├── parse
│   ├── app.rs
│   ├── extern_interrupt.rs
│   ├── hardware_task.rs
│   ├── idle.rs
│   ├── init.rs
│   ├── late_resource.rs
│   ├── local.rs
│   ├── software_task.rs
│   └── util.rs
├── parse.rs
├── tests
│   ├── multi.rs
│   └── single.rs
└── tests.rs

2 directories, 19 files
```

Listing 3.2: Structure of rtfm-syntax

has a port targeting cortex-a-rtic[20].

With this in mind, the analyze and check stages found within cortex-m-rtfm is thus platform dependent to cortex-m, as indicated by the name.

3.3.3 Code path through the framework

With cortex-m-ric acting as the root of the project, it is mainly a wrapper providing the test suite and examples. The majority of work happens within cortex-m-rtfm-macros which is a workspace member, located in the subfolder macros. cortex-m-rtfm-macros provides the Rust attribute macro, which is used to preprocess the given input.

rtfm-syntax is used during this preprocessing stage and it performs syntax verification as well as analysis. The structured output and metadata gathered during the analysis stage is then returned back to cortex-m-rtfm-macros which then uses the codegen module to construct the code for output.

A manually created schematic overview of the above is found in Figure 3.4.

---

[20]

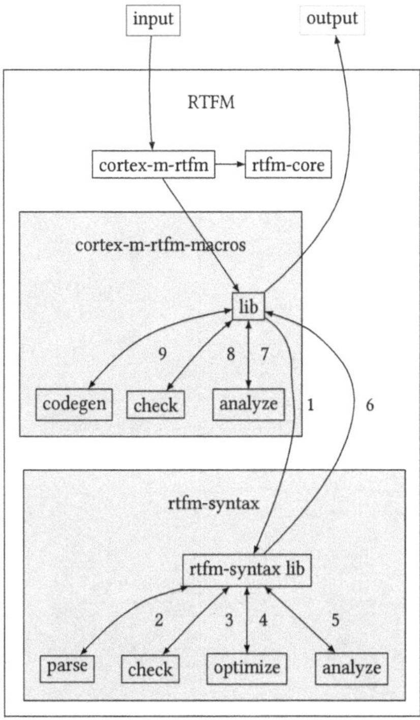

Figure 3.4: The software path through the RTFM framework

Starting from the input node, the code annotated with the #[app][21] macro provides the input. The number label on the edges indicate order of operation, thus
within rtfm-syntax the parse step is done first, followed by check, then optimize
and finally analyze before returning back to lib within cortex-m-rtfm-macros.

The logical structure consists of two major parts, as seen in Figure 3.4, the two
large areas with grey background; cortex-m-rtfm-macros and rtfm-syntax.

There is a clear path through the framework but it may not be obvious at first,
before building a model of the structure.

If the cortex-m-rtfm-macros crate is moved outside of the cortex-m-rtfm directory it is possible to work around the workspace limitation, and get cargo-deps to
produce some graphs. Since there are so many modules under codegen the graph
becomes very wide, but with some tweaking and using the NEATO[22] engine it is
doable.

The command used to generate the structural overview:

```
rustup run nightly cargo modules --enable-edition-2018 graph\
  --external --conditional --types > structure.dot
```

The output is found in Figure 3.5.

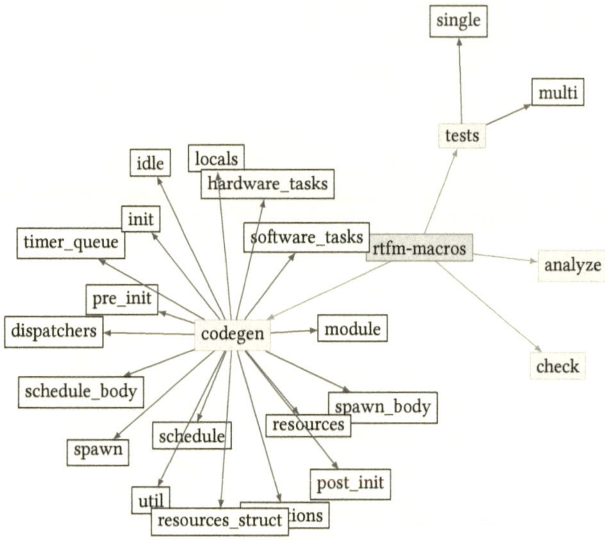

Figure 3.5: Structural layout of cortex-m-rtfm-macros crate

3.4   Future structural layout of RTIC

This section discusses some ideas and potential ways how to structure the framework to gain the desired extensibility and improve the issue presented in section 1.3.

3.4.1   Modules instead of CONST

With the development of the Rust language comes more ergonomic solutions and possibilities to improve software.

One such example arrived with the Rust compiler version 1.42.0 made stable 2020-03-10, thanks to the method of Rust releases both the **nightly** and **beta** was available before this to enable testing. With this release method the feature has at least two times six weeks exposure and testing before usable on the stable release channel.

The specific feature was implemented in pull request 64273[23] and eventually stabilised in Rust `1.42.0` allows placing Rust attributes on modules. Previously without this support a workaround was implemented using a constant, `const`, value instead since `const`s supported attributes. The use of the attribute is to invoke the `cortex-m-rtic-macros`.

The workaround is shown in Listing 3.3 and the now available normal rust module in Listing 3.4.

```
1   #[rtfm::app(device = lm3s6965)]
2   const APP: () = {
3     <code here>
4   };
```

Listing 3.3: `const` acting as a module

```
1   #[rtfm::app(device = lm3s6965)]
2   mod app {
3     <code here>
4   }
```

Listing 3.4: A proper Rust module supporting attributes

There are some additional details apart from the syntax change. Since the `const` `APP` workaround was non-standard the usage could freely be decided in order fit the requirements. Now with a proper Rust module it would be unexpected and bad if they did not behave like standard Rust modules. Before with the workaround any arbitrary user code was not allowed within the `const` `APP` acting as a module, but by implementing Rust modules this must be supported.

With this support for having arbitrary code within the module the ability to introduce parsers for custom new syntax arises since both "standard RTIC" and user provided code are input to the attribute macro.

3.4.2 Removal of multi-core support

The multi-core support is an experimental feature, it is feature-gated and requires the *nightly* Rust compiler. It is uncertain how widespread usage was, but the impact on the RTIC codebase is without doubt tangible.

When studying the source of `rtic-syntax` a pattern emerges where the source code structure is similar to what is found in Listing 3.5.

```
1   < cut >
2   if cores == 1 {
3       // the single core will initialize all the late resourcesA
4       if let Some(init) = app.inits.get(&0) {
5           if !init.returns_late_resources {
6               return Err(parse::Error::new(
7                   init.name.span(),
8                   "late resources exist so `#[init]` must return `init::LateResources`",
9               ));
10          }
11      } else {
12          return Err(parse::Error::new(
13              Span::call_site(),
14              "late resources exist so a `#[init]` function must be defined",
15          ));
16      }
17  } else {
18      // this core will initialize the "rest" of late resources
19      let mut rest = None;
20      // Continues for 56 more lines with a double nested for-loops and conditionals
21      < cut MULTI CORE >
22  }
23  < cut >
```

Listing 3.5: Example of multi-core complexity in `rtic-syntax` including annotation

The code listing is not complete, in the `else` case, for multi-core 56 lines were omitted, in contrast to the 13 lines in the single core case, excluding my annotation.

This pattern was observed throughout the codebase, the much more complex case of supporting multiple cores detracted from the readability and core functionality of the framework since the code overwhelmingly dealt with the special cases introduced by having multi-core support.

The two crates related to multi-core now being part of the `cortex-m-rtic` workspace would be removed with the possibility that they are reimplemented as an extension in separate crates instead. In addition to this, the tests related to multi-core would also be removed.

The current structure having homogeneous and heterogeneous as workspace members is well done. The issue is that the complexity required to support the multi-core use-case is also present within both `cortex-m-rtic-macros` and `rtic-syntax`.

3.4.3 Exchangeable modules

The purpose of having a modular and extendable design of the framework is to reduce the risk of fork divergence by making code changes local and concentrated and easily replaced with custom modules.

Such custom modules could easily be developed by copying on of the regular modules, modifying it, and then import that custom module under the same name, taking the place of the regular module.

In contrast, if the user has to do many small changes spread over a large set of files, the risk for complex merge conflicts during updates from upstream is large. The way `cortex-m-rtic-macros` and `rtic-syntax` are structured now, as seen in Figure 3.4, the ideal place for the user to make modifications is within each crates primary library.

Since that library sequentially calls each module it becomes easy to use these modules as a singular unit, where it is possible to fully replaceable a module or to appended a new module somewhere along the execution path.

A sufficiently flexible API design between the modules allowing for example the addition of fields holding extra metadata gathered from some new analysis step the user needs would be required. See Figure 3.6 for a visualisation of the current code path through rtic-syntax.

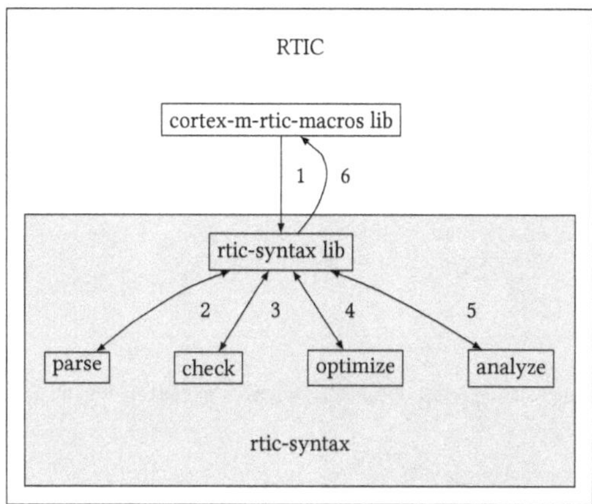

Figure 3.6: The software path through rtic-syntax

First step done as part of rtic-syntax is to use the parse module, to build an internal representation of the user code. It is represented as a TokenStream[24] which is a sequence of token trees. This sequence of tokens is then passed to the check module which does what the name suggests, runs additional verification against the user input and prevents model-breaking input not caught by the parse module. Next is optimize which compresses the user-provided priority levels into a continuous sequence of integers. Followed by that the analyze step is where the largest part of work is done.

A large chunk of the analysis code is related to multi-core, and with only the single-core parts in mind it is not as overwhelming.

A lot of the code also deals with the declaration of structs and enums which gets combined into the final output. For version v0.4.0 of rtic-syntax the Source lines of code (SLOC) for whole of analyze is 712 SLOC, the strucs, enums and impls for the structs accounts for 217 SLOC.

Example of modification

A potential scenario would be that a user wants to add an extra field on tasks describing some property of that task, let us call it deadline. One way to achieve this

is to extend `parse` to accept the new attribute which then can be placed on the task
at will.

The parser then must do something with this information it now can gather, it
will be handled by the function `task_args`, the function signature can be studied in
Listing 3.6.

```
1   fn task_args(
2       tokens: TokenStream2,
3       settings: &Settings,
4   ) -> parse::Result<Either<HardwareTaskArgs, SoftwareTaskArgs>> {
5       (|input: ParseStream<'_>| -> parse::Result<Either<HardwareTaskArgs, SoftwareTaskArgs>> {
6           if input.is_empty() {
7               return Ok(Either::Right(SoftwareTaskArgs::default()));
8           }
9
10          let mut binds = None;
11          let mut capacity = None;
12          let mut priority = None;
13          let mut resources = None;
14
15          < cut >
```

Listing 3.6: Overview of the `rtic-syntax::parse` function signature

The function parsing task arguments expects a TokenStream and the `settings`
struct which contains what is given directly via the app-macro. The function returns
either a struct named `HardwareTaskArgs` or `SoftwareTaskArgs`, depending on the
input encountered.

The `HardwareTaskArgs` struct already has a special feature making it *extendable*,
it is possible to add more fields to the structure during compilation.

In order to provide a custom parse module, the user would then make a copy
of the current parse module, name it `parsecustom` and modify that to achieve the
desired functionality. Then in order to use the new module, instead of importing the
old `parse` with the Rust use declaration `parsecustom` would take its place. To make it
even more seamless, it is possible to use it under another name, so `use parsecustom
as parse` would essentially replace `parse` and no other changes would be necessary
since the paths to `parse` are still valid.

See Figure 3.7 for a structural layout of the above suggestion.

Then somewhere in the later stages of the code path the user could use their new
fields.

This way of introducing new modules to the code could be mirrored for `cortex-
m-rtic-macros` as well, and by changing the required parts a custom solution with
minimal changes of the framework itself could be achieved.

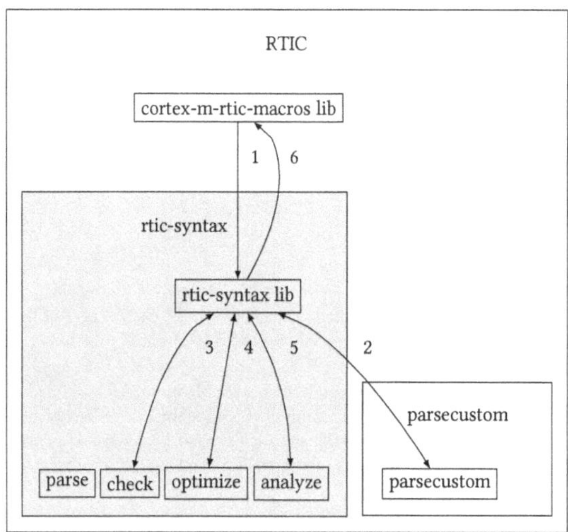

Figure 3.7: An alternative software path through `rtic-syntax`, providing a custom parsing module

3.5 Continuous Integration

There are two primary ways to verify correctness of software, static verification using formal methods to show correctness, or dynamic verification which is what most people call *testing*.

Both have their strengths and weaknesses, but ideally one would combine both[25] to get the best verification achievable.

Building on top of methods which are themselves proven via formal methods does not automatically imply that your implementation is correct. There is always a risk of implementation dependent bugs or even language or toolchain introduced bugs.

There has been much written on the subject of testing and verification and the focus of this thesis is not about formal methods. Dynamic verification (testing) during the implementation of new features and modification of code structure is an invaluable tool.

Because without proper tests any code modification could introduce unnoticed side effects causing errors.

To further reduce the risk of introducing bugs during the merge of modified code a deterministic way of merging code is to enforce that the test suit passes before the merge happens. It may be tempting to think "I'll fix this later", but it is easy to forget. Bors[26] is a tool that improves the way merges to the master branch are handled. By requiring passing CI before the merge is done, and it can combine multiple merges into one CI test run to speed up the merge process. If one change introduces some breaking change the tests are rerun to isolate the change which breaks testing and that is reported on the related pull request. So Bors helps you not forgetting those small fixes by ensuring they are done right away.

The benefit is that every commit which lands in the master branch is then fully tested and should work as intended.

3.5.1 Travis CI

The RTFM framework use Travis CI[27] but the performance is not ideal.

The original Travis CI setup which was created in the early stages of the framework development has only been added and extended to, it is possible to optimise the current CI suite further.

Travis jobs are specially annotated shell scripts running for defined `targets` allowing parallelism. For example, running the tests for the `thumbv6m-none-eabi` target at the same time as the job for `x86_64-unknown-linux-gnu` is running. See Listing 3.7 for an abbreviated Travis configuration showing different targets used in RTFM.

```yaml
language: rust

matrix:
  include:
    # NOTE used to build docs on successful merges to master
    - env: TARGET=x86_64-unknown-linux-gnu

      # MSRV
    - env: TARGET=thumbv7m-none-eabi
      rust: 1.36.0
      if: (branch = staging OR branch = trying) OR \
          (type = pull_request AND branch = master)

    - env: TARGET=thumbv6m-none-eabi
      if: (branch = staging OR branch = trying) OR \
          (type = pull_request AND branch = master)

    - env: TARGET=thumbv7m-none-eabi
      if: (branch = staging OR branch = trying) OR \
          (type = pull_request AND branch = master)
< cut >
script:
  - bash ci/script.sh
< cut >
```

Listing 3.7: A trimmed `.travis.yml` for `cortex-m-rtfm`

The `script:` key informs Travis which script or command it should run. To get the desired functionality `script.sh` uses conditionals to control if parts are to be executed or not since the same script gets run for every defined target. Travis passes the information given in the `matrix` as environment variables. Then they can be used as seen in Listing 3.8.

```
< cut >
if [ $T = x86_64-unknown-linux-gnu ]; then
        if [[ $TRAVIS_RUST_VERSION == 1.*.* ]]; then
        < cut >
```

Listing 3.8: How Travis do conditional execution

Travis CI pricing

The pricing model for Travis CI has been generous towards open-source since their creation in 2011, but in early 2019 they were bought by Idera[28] and a few weeks after the acquisition lots of the original Travis CI staff were laid off[29] causing a concern for the future availability of Travis CI within the open-source community.

3.5.2   New contender: GitHub Actions

GitHub Actions (GHA) was introduced[30] with CI support in late 2019. There was talk within the Embedded Rust community and an investigation whether to switch from Travis to GitHub Actions was beneficial. For more details, see the pull request for the `svd2rust` tool where GitHub Actions replaces Travis[31].

GitHub Actions has a declarative syntax in comparison to Travis's imperative scripts. Different styles but equally capable. Preference or experience with other tools using a similar configuration style such as Docker[32] are beneficial.

See Listing 3.9 for an example of the declarative nature of GitHub Actions, here installing the community[33] provided GitHub Action `toolchain` which installs and configures the Rust toolchain, followed by `cargo` which runs the desired cargo command.

```yaml
< cut >
jobs:
  # Run cargo fmt --check, includes macros/
  style:
    name: style
    runs-on: ubuntu-20.04
    steps:
      - name: Checkout
        uses: actions/checkout@v1

      - name: Install Rust
        uses: actions-rs/toolchain@v1
        with:
          profile: minimal
          toolchain: stable
          override: true
          components: rustfmt

      - name: cargo fmt --check
        uses: actions-rs/cargo@v1
        with:
          command: fmt
          args: --all -- --check
< cut >
```

Listing 3.9: GitHub Actions declarative configuration

GitHub Actions pricing

The pricing model[34] for GitHub Actions for organisations became "gratis"[35] on 2020-04-14, thus making it a viable competitor to Travis for public repositories. This free plan includes 2000 actions minutes per month and up to 500MB och GitHub Packages storage.

The free plan accommodates 20 concurrent jobs simultaneously, surpassing this limit, jobs are queued and run as soon as one of the already started jobs are finished.

In order to reduce the time taken for each run it is advisable to split the test suite into similarly time-consuming jobs.

Chapter 4

Implementation

This chapter describes some changes implemented in order to approach the end goal of increased extensibility of the RTIC framework.

4.1 Module instead of CONST

Thought to be an easy modification, the implementation of `mod_const` turned out to be a bit more involved. The Request For Comments (RFC)[1] describes the story.

The change led to two "bonus" improvements.

Since Rust modules[2] are well defined in their behaviour in contrast to the workaround `const APP: () = { < cut > }` constant of "unit" type it is easier for the user to know what to expect. To change to a module Rust expectations must be met, one such expectation is that the content within a module should be modifiable. The previous implementation only accepted the defined RTFM keywords and attributes in addition to the statically named structure `Resources`.

To simplify parsing and at the same time gain more consistency in the user interface the syntax for defining the resource struct was changed to an attribute. Thus the syntax became fully symmetric and now all RTIC special annotations became attributes: `#[task]`, `#[init]`, `#[idle]`, `#[resources]`, `#[task_local]` and `#[lock_free]`.

For a before and after example see Listing 4.1 and Listing 4.2, which describes the change in syntax. There are also more changes in relation to symmetry, not directly related to `mod_const` changes, but in latest alpha release `#[init]` is also symmetric always returning `init::LateResources`[3].

Now with the attribute `#[resources]` determining what becomes the "resources struct", the name of the struct does not have to be "`Resources`" anymore, the only requirement is that struct identifiers should be formatted with CamelCase, as done in Listing 4.2, changing it to `StuffStuffStuff` is accepted.

```rust
< cut >
#[rtfm::app(device = lm3s6965)]
const APP: () = {
    struct Resources {
        // A resource
        #[init(0)]
        shared: u32,
    }

    #[init]
    fn init(_: init::Context) {
        < cut >
    }

    #[idle]
    fn idle(_cx: idle::Context) -> ! {
        < cut >
    }

    // `shared` can be accessed from this context
    #[task(binds = UART0, resources = [shared])]
    fn uart0(cx: uart0::Context) {
        < cut >
    }
    < cut >
};
```

Listing 4.1: RTFM v0.5.1: Excerpt from examples/resource.rs

```rust
< cut >
#[rtic::app(device = lm3s6965)]
mod app {
    #[resources]
    struct StuffStuffStuff {
        // A resource
        #[init(0)]
        shared: u32,
    }

    #[init]
    fn init(_: init::Context) -> init::LateResources {
        < cut >
        init::LateResources {}
    }

    // `shared` cannot be accessed from this context
    #[idle]
    fn idle(_cx: idle::Context) -> ! {
        < cut >
    }

    // `shared` can be accessed from this context
    #[task(binds = UART0, resources = [shared])]
    fn uart0(mut cx: uart0::Context) {
        < cut >
    }
    < cut >
}
```

Listing 4.2: RTIC v0.6.0-alpha.0: Excerpt from examples/resource.rs

Rust modules also behaves a certain way in relation to the namespace and the need for use-statements to access resources outside of a module arises. The output from the RTIC macro thus must ensure that these expectations are met. This is directly dependent on the ability to insert arbitrary code since the user need to provide such use-statements like in any other Rust module.

The code provided by the user must be stored somewhere to be passed along to later stages. Two Rust vec[4]s were used to store the user code within the App struct.

Listing 4.3 show how all code not matching any of the defined match arms but the _ branch, which is a catch-all to handle such "other" cases[5] is rejected with an informative error, highlighting the "misplaced" code.

Listing 4.4 show how the two new cases are stored into the new vectors, one for use-statements and one for any arbitrary user code. The reason they are separated is to ease generation of special support structures which do not need the user code but do need the use-statements.

```
1   < cut >
2     for mut item in input.items {
3         match item {
4           < cut >
5           _ => {
6             return Err(parse::Error::new(
7                 item.span(),
8                 "this item must live outside the `#[app]` module",
9             ));
10          }
11      }
12    < cut >
```

Listing 4.3: rtic-syntax v0.4.0: Excerpt from src/parse/app.rs

```
1   < cut >
2     for mut item in input.items {
3         match item {
4           < cut >
5           Item::Use(itemuse_) => {
6               // Store the user provided use-statements
7               user_imports.push(itemuse_.clone());
8           }
9           _ => {
10              // Anything else within the module should not make any difference
11              user_code.push(item.clone());
12          }
13      }
14    < cut >
```

Listing 4.4: rtic-syntax v0.5.0-alpha.0: Excerpt from src/parse/app.rs

Implementing mod_const hit a road-block when multi-core tests failed unexpectedly. The syntax for single and multi-core does not differ, but errors about undefined items not related to the direct changes made for some interesting debugging deep-dives.

It turns out that some of these support structures were not generated at all. Two clear paths forward emerged, one where the alpha-quality multi-core was fixed to ensure all tests passed with mod_const functionality or the other where multi-core support was removed and the already functioning single-core implementation could be merged to master.

The decision was made to not try to fix multi-core but to focus on removing multi-core and simplify the codebase and then return to mod_const.

4.2   Improving CI

Since the developers in Rust Embedded Working Group (wg)[6] were considering GitHub Actions it made sense to at least get a feeling for the tool. By July the wg added GitHub Actions to the setup instructions[7] for newly added repositories, giving a recommended configuration for GHA.

4.2.1   Porting Travis CI to GitHub Actions

From the first failed GitHub Actions job on 2020-05-31 to a merged Pull Request[8] 4 days later, fully implementing the current Travis CI attests to the quality of the documentation, the multitude of written guides, blog-posts and success stories from other in a similar situation.

The way of using pre-packaged "Actions" was convenient and effective, but with GHA not limited to only that, custom scripting directly copied from the Travis CI configuration works as one would expect. The resources provided by actions-rs[9] proved invaluable when it comes to working with a Rust project. From code examples to functionality provided, it was a good experience. Travis CI felt a bit more like a "Do It Yourself" (DIY) solution in the sense that it was harder to abstract away basic functionality into pre-packaged "actions" like GHA had achieved. Certainly doable, the support for BASH functions as in any other BASH script is there. On a positive note for Travis, before the actions became understandable and the syntax made sense, the Travis CI BASH script felt right at home.

See section1.3.2 CI Testing and tools for Travis CI performance for cortex-m-rtic.

First improvement was to use a pre-built[10] version of the static site generator for the documentation called mdBook[11], this was backported to Travis CI to cut down testing time.

Satisfied with the stability and functionality of GHA, Bors the build bot was re-configured[12] to use GHA and Travis CI was decommissioned.

The full configurations for both tools can be studied on GitHub:

- Old v0.5.1 Travis CI configuration[13]

- GitHub Actions configuration[14]

To optimise for speed the test suite was split into separate jobs, both to facilitate "fail early" but also to fully utilise the 20 available concurrent jobs the GitHub free plan allows[15].

4.3 Renaming RTFM to RTIC

After consensus was reached on a new name[16] for the framework the task to do the actual rename remained.

Manually changing all occurrences of the old name would have been a overly time-consuming task, thus using tools for the job was a given. Turning to a tool written in Rust named sd[17] with functionality similar to GNU sed[18], to search and replace text. sd version 0.1.0 was released on 24th of December 2018, in contrast to the considerably older sed making its first appearance in 1974[19].

sd together with the find replacement fd written in Rust, turned out to be an powerful combination.

The script in Listing 4.5 should be placed outside of the working directory containing the files to be rename else the script also will be modified. An alternative solution is to add the argument `--exclude rename-rtfm-rtic.bash` to fd.

```
#!/bin/bash


sd -f c RTFM RTIC $(fd --type file)
sd -f c rtfm rtic $(fd --type file)

sd -f c 'Real-Time For the Masses' \
        'Real-Time Interrupt-driven Concurrency' \
        $(fd --type file)

sd -f c 'Real-Time for The Masses' \
        'Real-Time Interrupt-driven Concurrency' \
        $(fd --type file)

sd -f c 'Real Time For the Masses' \
        'Real-Time Interrupt-driven Concurrency' \
        $(fd --type file)
```

Listing 4.5: rename-rtfm-rtic.bash: script renaming RTFM to RTIC

Note that the duplication of lines are to handle permutations of the project name found throughout the source and documentation. With or without hyphen, capitalisation also varied. With the acronym *RTFM*, the intended capitalisation was "Real-Time For the Masses".

4.4 Removal of multi-core support

RTFM were rebuilt around multi-core support as part of version v0.5.0 and thus the data structures were chosen with this in mind.

4.4.1 `rtic-syntax`

Starting in `rtic-syntax` and using the test-suite to verify each step anything related to `core` was removed. It quickly became hard to keep track of all the changes required in order to make the test suite and `cargo check` happy.

After an attempted change from HashMap[20] to HashSet[21] data structures turns out HashSet does not provide a way to get a mutable reference, the reason is well described in the [documentation]:

> It is a logic error for a key to be modified in such a way that the key's hash, as determined by the Hash trait, or its equality, as determined by the Eq trait, changes while it is in the map. This is normally only possible through Cell, RefCell, global state, I/O, or unsafe code.

Thus it is a design decision in order to uphold the Rust memory safety guarantees and since there are other data-types providing the `.get_mut()` functionality required this prompted a pause and further thought.

This first attempt to remove multi-core was a bit too aggressive since the data structures also needing to change required more thorough design decisions, thinking through what functionality was required and what was available for each `std::collections` Rust provides.

Changing the strategy to taking smaller steps instead fared better, since the tools available such as rust-analyzer[22] are able to support the debugging of type incompatibilities and missing fields along the way.

Without touching the actual multi-core implementation, the first step was starting at the input stage of parsing by removing the ability to give the `core` argument to the app macro. In effect disabling the possibility to use multi-core.

Next step was to remove all the parts of `check` dealing with multi-core. This was seamless since this check is not a dependency for any other stage in regards to multi-core. It would be possible to write faulty multi-core since there were no checks, but that was taken care of by the prior removal of the ability to activate multi-core support.

Then with the help of rust-analyzer integrated into the IDE, the struct item `core` was removed from the structs `InitArgs` and `IdleArgs`. Then the general procedure was the following:

Rust-analyzer indicates an error about the missing `core` field. Then jump to the location where the error is reported, resolve the error by removing the use of the field and see what rust-analyzer finds next, repeat until no more errors. Proceed by removing another multi-core related item and let rust-analyzer guide you through it just as before.

Previously each core had their own separate `idle` and `init`, with multi-core removed `idle` and `init` will now be singular, but the convenience features provided by

Vector[23] and the ability to check if there exists an `init` or `idle` instead of manually implementing it for the struct.

Additionally, vectors provide ready to use iterators. There is a possibility to use `std::iter::once` to simulate the required iterator, but combined with the use of `.first()` method it became more ergonomic to use the vector as a wrapper and get the iterator from `vec`.

Often found in idiomatic Rust code, iterators[24] are a powerful way to operate over data sets and are heavily used in the framework. In combination with the iterator a large set of functions providing operations like `filter` and conditionals allows for even more powerful ways of both modifying and conditionally returning only desired parts.

```
1      < cut >
2      let mut inits = Vec::new();
3      < cut >
4      for mut item in input.items {
5          match item {
6              Item::Fn(mut item) => {
7                  let span = item.sig.ident.span();
8                  if let Some(pos) = item
9                      .attrs
10                     .iter()
11                     .position(|attr| util::attr_eq(attr, "init"))
12                 {
13                     let args = InitArgs::parse(item.attrs.remove(pos).tokens)?;
14
15                     // If an init function already exists, error
16                     if !inits.is_empty() {
17                         return Err(parse::Error::new(
18                             span,
19                             "`#[init]` function must appear at most once",
20                         ));
21                     }
22
23                     check_ident(&item.sig.ident)?;
24
25                     inits.push(Init::parse(args, item)?);
26                 } else if let Some(pos) = item
27                     < cut >
```

Listing 4.6: How the #[init] function is parsed

In Listing 4.6 an excerpt showing how `inits` at most will contain one init by using `if !inits.is_empty()` to check for conflicts in case the user defines more than one #[init].

Row 8 in the Listing showcases the usage of an iterator, by iterating through all the attributes `attr` on `item`. `.position()`[25] takes a closure and by evaluating if that closure returns `true` or `false` the result will either be `Some(index)` or `None`. The closure `|attr| util::attr_eq(attr, "init")` checks if the attribute equals to `"init"`. Thus only functions with the attribute `"init"` are returned into `if let Some(pos) = item` where the rest of the code within the curly braces (row 12 to 21) is run in case the return value from the iterator is `Some(pos)`, where `pos` is the name of the variable available inside the curly braces containing the index returned.

If the function is properly parsed by `InitArgs::parse()` it is added to `inits`. In case multiple functions are annotated with `#[init]` the error "#[init] function must appear at most once" alerts the user that having multiple init functions is not permissible.

The multi-core implementation relied heavily on HashMap and HashSet as well as BTreeMap, primarily keyed on `core`. With `core` being removed there is nothing to key on, and since the meaning of `core` is also lost either a HashSet or a Vector will do the job in most cases. At times it was possible to remove altogether, when the data structure was wrapping another iterator.

Thus the primary data structure modifications needed were resolved by replacing a keyed collection with an non-keyed one.

For the full diff see the pull request #27[26]

When all the tests were passing and all references to `core` were removed, work continued with `cortex-m-rtic`.

4.4.2 `cortex-m-rtic`

After deleting the `heterogeneous` and `homogeneous` workspace member crates the work to adapt `cortex-m-rtic` to the changes in `rtic-syntax` could begin.

Running the test suite for the first time caused an avalanche of errors and complaints about missing fields in most data structures.

Rust-analyzer were used as described previously and slowly but surely the count of errors dwindled.

Throughout the crate a lot of multi-core specific code could be eliminated, resulting in a much slimmer and to the point implementation. The check and analysis steps were considerably trimmed. The old version of `analyze.rs` used the following data-structure to describe the interrupts.

```rust
/// Extend the upstream `Analysis` struct with our field
pub struct Analysis {
    parent: P<analyze::Analysis>,
    pub interrupts: BTreeMap<Core, BTreeMap<Priority, Ident>>,
}
```

Listing 4.7: Old data-structure for `interrupts`.

```rust
/// Extend the upstream `Analysis` struct with our field
pub struct Analysis {
    parent: P<analyze::Analysis>,
    pub interrupts: BTreeMap<Priority, Ident>,
}
```

Listing 4.8: New data-structure for `interrupts`.

---

[26]<https://github.com/rtic-rs/rtic-syntax/pull/27/files>

Listing 4.7 and Listing 4.8 shows how the way to describe `interrupts` changed with the removal of multi-core. The actual interrupt is a `BTreeMap` keyed on `Priority` and storing an `Ident`. This was then wrapped in another `BTreeMap` keyed on `Core`. Since there is no need for `Core` anymore, the outer `BTreeMap` collection keyed on `Core` could be removed.

Simplifications similar to these were scattered throughout the codebase, for the full diff see pull request #355[27].

4.5   Structural layout of RTIC

This part, as noted in section 1.4 Delimitations, has not been implemented due to scope changes in relation to the new set of responsibilities associated with being a core developer of the framework.

Additionally, the implementation of the improvements listed in prior sections all simplifies the codebase, making a change in the structure a less complex task.

With multi-core support removed the ability to get a proper structural overview is improved, which in turn aids in the process of both designing and later implementing the new structure. In a sense then the success of a structure change depends on the cleanup of the current state since the overly complex multi-core capable structure presents a greater challenge.

Chapter 5

Evaluation

This chapter starts with a discussion about the way development and peer review is done within the RTIC open-source community, followed by the results achieved in regard to the problem definitions.

5.1 RTIC open-source community

The RTIC community is modeled after the Rust community, focusing on transparency, openness and being welcoming to all. User feedback and the diverse set of use-cases of the framework allows for extensive testing and helps improve the overall quality.

5.1.1 CI and reviews

When working with the codebase, when the local tools like cargo-check and rust-analyzer are satisfied, next tool in line is the CI system.

When the CI system is pleased, the next in row to go through the code is the reviewer. The reviewer is more focused on the design decisions, the reasoning behind the implementation and that correctness should be preserved. Since the CI test suite is not perfect, it is really important to do proper reviews of all code.

Our brain is sometimes unhelpful with aggressive "autocomplete" if you know what you have written or recognize the patterns enough. There may be erroneous comments or other small or large things which the compiler did not complain about, which passed by CI unnoticed and could end up littering in the code for a long time going forward unless noticed by the reviewer or implementer.

5.1.2 User feedback

Early adopters and testers may also notice and question peculiar implementations or ugly hacks.

The practice of doing software design beforehand also helps improve the resulting code, since by requiring that one present the whole solution other can provide insight into potential draw-backs or suggest alternative methods to improve the overall quality. This design phase is done via the Request For Comments (RFC)[1] where the process is the same as for the Rust language, described in full in the Rust RFCs book[2].

Since RTIC does not have the same intense volume of incoming RFCs like the Rust language has, the process is a bit more relaxed, for now there are no robots involved, the process is done manually. But the core concepts are the same, and when the ideas proposed have time to mature and receive feedback from other community members, the level of quality is raised since the combined knowledge often surpasses that of individuals due to differing past experiences and specialisations.

The weekly meetings allows for dealing with problems, showcasing solutions and planning the future direction of the project. Discussion is held publicly with the hope that the collective knowledge, similarly like for the RFCs, found within the community provides valuable insights which might have been overlooked.

Since all these steps of review and collaboration aims to raise the quality of work as high as possible, a completed merge is considered a success.

It may happen that unforeseen consequences or external dependencies cause breakage, but as pragmatic problem-solvers the focus will be on solving the issues at hand instead of placing blame.

5.2 Regular Rust module instead of custom const `APP`

The feature was implemented in rtic-syntax[3] cortex-m-rtic PR#368[4] and fully implements the desired functionality as described in section 4.1.

The majority of changes consists of updating all examples and test to the new syntax.

For `cortex-m-rtic` the change also included modifying the test setup to remove tests for the old Minimum Supported Rust Version (MSRV) `1.36.0` which does not support attributes on modules. With the next version of the framework another method for specifying MSRV will be used, targeting the current stable.

Annotating the Resource-struct with an `#[resources]` attribute instead of a fixed name also allows for custom user-code within the `app` module. Something which previously was forbidden. This opens up for extensions to the framework. With a regular Rust module there are new possibilities in regards to code structure. It will be interesting to see what kind of use-cases people within the community can come up with.

5.3 CI improvements

Implementing GitHub Actions has also been done for `rtic-examples` and `rtic-syntax`. Same procedure, porting the existing Travis CI solution by using GitHub Actions from `actions-rs`.

A selection of notable pull requests related to making the CI perform as optimal as possible.

- Testing GHA v0.1[5]
    - The introduction of GitHub Actions CI to `cortex-m-rtic`.
- Use statically compiled mdbook[6]
    - Drastically improved the performance of CI by not having to compile mdBook from source.

- Combine publish, docs and build into one GHA workflow[7]
    - Major structural changes in CI, job overview became much better.
- Enable caching for Github Actions[8]
    - Reduce the running time by caching build artifacts between runs.
- The stable book should be built from branch[9]
    - Separate the dev docs from the released versions.
- Separate example check and run-pass tests[10]
    - Using all 20 available concurrent jobs reduces runtime.

The current average run-time for the CI suite is about 4 minutes compared with the average run-time for Travis CI which was 15 minutes, we can conclude that we have 3.75 times quicker average CI-runtime after the switch. Additionally, the integration of GitHub and GitHub Actions is without doubt better than what is possible with an external CI suite such as Travis CI.

5.4 RTIC onwards

The total change amounting to 522 modified lines, details visible in the following pull requests:

- cortex-m-rtic[11] changed: 454 lines
- rtic-syntax[12] changed: 29 lines
- rtic-core[13] changed: 18 lines
- rtic-examples[14] changed: 21 lines

Now rtfm.rs[15] redirects to rtic.rs[16] and the name of the GitHub organisation also reflects the name change. The reception of the name change has been overwhelmingly positive.

5.5 The impact of removing multi-core support

Looking first at `rtic-syntax`, it is clear that the overall size of the repository and codebase saw a significant change with the removal of multi-core support.

Using the code statistics program Tokei[17] a baseline is established in Figure 5.1 and then comparing this to Figure 5.2 which is directly after the merged multiremove PR. Figure 5.3 describes the current latest state when writing this of the `rtic-syntax` master branch.

Looking specifically at the columns "Code" and "Comments" an interesting result is to be noted, the amount of code has been significantly reduced while the drop in number of comments has not seen such a sizable reduction.

This stems from how the process of working through the multiremove implementation required understanding of the code, allowing me to document and verify the validity of current comments.

```
rtic-syntax on  HEAD (4a6bc63) [$?] is  v0.4.0 via  v1.47.0
) tokei
===============================================================================
 Language            Files        Lines        Code     Comments       Blanks
===============================================================================
 Markdown                3          106           0           65           41
 Shell                   1           37          30            2            5
 TOML                    2           44          38            0            6
-------------------------------------------------------------------------------
 Rust                   80         4942        4060          138          744
 |- Markdown            10          217           0          209            8
 (Total)                           5159        4060          347          752
===============================================================================
 Total                  86         5346        4128          414          804
===============================================================================
```

Figure 5.1: rtic-syntax before multiremove

```
rtic-syntax on  HEAD (2721cc1) [$?] is  v0.4.0 via  v1.47.0
) tokei
===============================================================================
 Language            Files        Lines        Code     Comments       Blanks
===============================================================================
 Markdown                3          106           0           65           41
 Shell                   1           37          30            2            5
 TOML                    2           44          38            0            6
-------------------------------------------------------------------------------
 Rust                   65         3718        3015          114          589
 |- Markdown             9          187           0          181            6
 (Total)                           3905        3015          295          595
===============================================================================
 Total                  71         4092        3083          362          647
===============================================================================
```

Figure 5.2: rtic-syntax after multiremove

```
rtic-syntax on  master [$?] is  v0.5.0-alpha.0 via  v1.47.0
) tokei
===============================================================================
 Language            Files        Lines        Code     Comments       Blanks
===============================================================================
 Markdown                3          140           0           85           55
 Shell                   1           37          30            2            5
 TOML                    2           44          38            0            6
-------------------------------------------------------------------------------
 Rust                   66         3671        2956          126          589
 |- Markdown            12          167           0          163            4
 (Total)                           3838        2956          289          593
===============================================================================
 Total                  72         4059        3024          376          659
===============================================================================
```

Figure 5.3: rtic-syntax as of November 2020

```
cortex-m-rtic on  HEAD (c103d46) [$?] is  v0.5.1 via  v1.47.0
) tokei
===============================================================================
 Language            Files        Lines         Code     Comments       Blanks
===============================================================================
 JSON                    1           79           79            0            0
 Markdown               43         4143            0         3116         1027
 Shell                   4          373          277           24           72
 TOML                    8          198          164            5           29
-------------------------------------------------------------------------------
 HTML                    1           15           13            2            0
 |- JavaScript           1            1            1            0            0
 (Total)                             16           14            2            0
-------------------------------------------------------------------------------
 Rust                   83         6003         4672          251         1080
 |- Markdown            57          410            0          312           98
 (Total)                           6413         4672          563         1178
===============================================================================
 Total                 140        11222         5206         3710         2306
===============================================================================
```

Figure 5.4: cortex-m-rtic before multiremove

```
cortex-m-rtic on  HEAD (7506bd8) [$?] is  v0.5.5 via  v1.47.0
) tokei
===============================================================================
 Language            Files        Lines         Code     Comments       Blanks
===============================================================================
 JSON                    1           79           79            0            0
 Markdown               42         4241            0         3183         1058
 Shell                   4          401          290           35           76
 TOML                    6          184          151            4           29
-------------------------------------------------------------------------------
 HTML                    1           15           13            2            0
 |- JavaScript           1            1            1            0            0
 (Total)                             16           14            2            0
-------------------------------------------------------------------------------
 Rust                   76         5132         3943          253          916
 |- Markdown            52          385            0          291           94
 (Total)                           5517         3943          544         1030
===============================================================================
 Total                 130        10438         4477         3768         2193
===============================================================================
```

Figure 5.5: cortex-m-rtic after multiremove

```
cortex-m-rtic on  master [$?] is  v0.5.5 via  v1.47.0 took 16s
) tokei
===============================================================================
 Language            Files        Lines         Code     Comments       Blanks
===============================================================================
 JSON                    1           79           79            0            0
 Shell                   4          401          290           35           76
 TOML                    6          198          156            4           30
-------------------------------------------------------------------------------
 HTML                    1           15           13            2            0
 |- JavaScript           1            1            1            0            0
 (Total)                             16           14            2            0
-------------------------------------------------------------------------------
 Markdown               42         4464            0         3328         1136
 |- Rust                 1            5            3            1            1
 (Total)                           4469            3         3329         1137
-------------------------------------------------------------------------------
 Rust                   84         5250         3987          262         1001
 |- Markdown            64          425            0          324          101
 (Total)                           5675         3987          586         1102
===============================================================================
 Total                 138        10830         4529         3956         2345
===============================================================================
```

Figure 5.6: cortex-m-rtic as of November 2020

The change in amount of code between Figure 5.2 and Figure 5.3 is not large in total code change. The number of comments in code has however increased while the documentation has been reduced. Improved interfaces requires less involved reading material for understanding.

Looking specifically at the `analyze` module found in `rtic-syntax` in section 3.4 the total SLOC count was given as 712, and the strucs, enums and impls for the structs accounted for 217 SLOC.

For the latest v0.5.0-alpha.0 the total SLOC are 412 and the data structures and impls account for 121 SLOC. The large decrease indicates that among other changes multi-core was totaling about half of the required structures and almost half of the implementation was specific for dealing with multi-core.

Moving on to `cortex-m-rtic` similar statistics can be observed, albeit not as large figures. The same procedure as above, first in Figure 5.4 the baseline is established, then in Figure 5.5 the stats directly after removal of multi-core support followed by Figure 5.6 showing the state as of November 2020 of the master branch.

The reduction in SLOC stemming from multiremove totals to 729 lines of code while the number of comments remained constant. The total number of files were reduced by 10.

The full development history and metadata can be studied in the following pull requests: rtic-syntax multiremove PR[18] and rtic multiremove PR[19].

See Figure A.1 and Figure A.2 in appendix A for the GitHub statistics for the pull request. In Git terminology one deleted line and one added line equals one change on that line. The sum of all changes is overwhelmingly negative, meaning more code was removed than introduced, reducing repository size and complexity.

The massive changes were reviewed which resulted in some minor changes, then they were merged to the master branch.

Something to note about these statistics are that they do not solely count code which has been removed, but all lines in files tracked by Git. Examples of other content which was removed includes multi-core tests and code examples.

Now with multi-core removed, among other things work on implementing `mod_const` could resume again.

5.6   Structural layout of RTIC; then and now

This section showcases the structural state of the repositories for the pre-release version of `cortex-m-rtic` version `v0.6.0-alpha.0` and `rtic-syntax` version `v0.5.0-alpha.0`.

As seen in the previous section, multiremove by itself caused a significant change in the structure, especially the overall size of the codebase.

5.6.1   `rtic-syntax`

Comparing Figure 5.7 and Figure 5.8 the only differences are the change of name from RTFM to RTIC, the removal of the `test/multi` module and `parse/extern_interrupt` has been merged into `parse/app`.

The overall structural layout has not changed much for `rtic-syntax`.

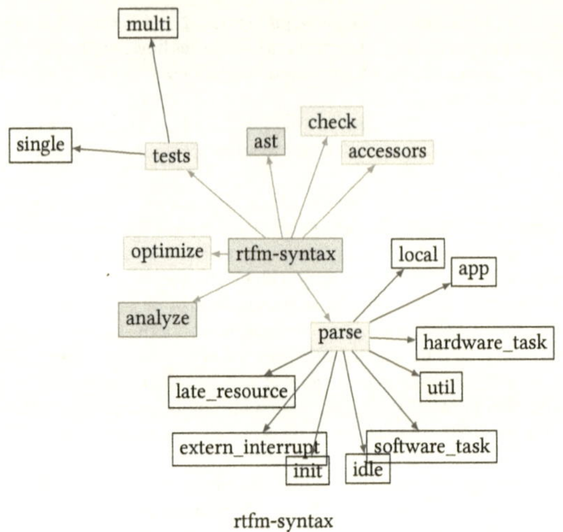

Figure 5.7: Structural overview of `rtic-syntax` v0.4.0

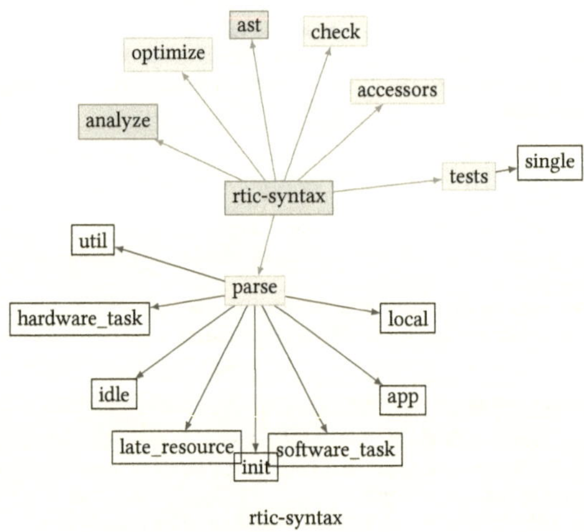

Figure 5.8: Structural overview of `rtic-syntax` v0.5.0-alpha.0

5.6.2 `cortex-m-rtic`

The dependency graph has not changed besides the removal of heterogeneous and
homogeneous and multi-core tests.

Comparing the change for `cortex-m-rtic` with the before case available in Figure 3.5 and after in Figure 5.9.

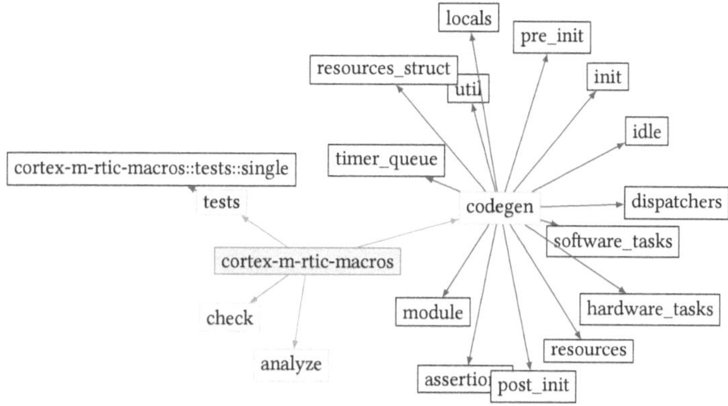

Figure 5.9: Structural layout of cortex-m-rtic-macros crate

Here the structural difference is primarily related to this pull request[20] where the
removal of multi-core allowed for easier implementation of a long awaited feature,
the ability to use RTIC tasks for callbacks, both spawned and scheduled. Now the
user also has the possibility to store a RTIC task.

The old way of spawning required you to have the context to spawn or queue,
limiting the spawning and queueing to RTIC tasks having access to that context.

The modules completely removed were:

- `codegen/schedule`
- `codegen/schedule_body`
- `codegen/spawn`
- `codegen/spawn_body`
- `tests/multi`

Yet again the overall structural change is minimal for `cortex-m-rtic`.

Chapter 6

Discussion

This chapter discusses the outcomes and different results presented in the previous chapter.

6.1 Managing an Open-Source project

When starting with the work for this thesis I did not anticipate that it would lead to joining an open-source project team as a core developer.

A large part of the work done during this thesis was related to furthering RTIC as an open-source project and being part of the Rust embedded community. In this section the open-source governance model, the tools available, common practices and conventions are discussed.

6.1.1 Rust project governance

Rust is known for their vibrant community and they are a source of inspiration in regard how to manage a open-source project. Their page on governance[1] details the practical aspects oft how the community builds Rust.

Their Request for Comments (RFC) method is a core principle of the Rust development philosophy, and all major decisions must go through this process. The Rust community has grown considerably since releasing Rust 1.0[2] in 2015 and as the Stackoverflow Developer Survey results[3] show, for the fifth year in a row Rust is voted the most loved language.

The scale at which Rust is now operating is impressive, and as the proverb goes: "imitation is the sincerest form of flattery".

6.1.2 RTIC project governance

Heavily inspired by Rust development model, RTIC implements the same RFC process[4] as Rust[5]. Since RTIC is built in Rust there is an overlap between the RTIC community and the Rust community in general and people trying to build embedded systems in Rust often find the RTIC project.

Maybe it happens the other way around too, that people looking for good to build real-time applications finds RTIC and then learns about Rust.

The core developer team leads the general direction and are responsible for making the decisions. Other members of the community are encouraged to also partake in all decisions, discussions and everything related to the project. This includes the ability to review pull requests, report issues, adding pull request and propose changes or request features via the RFC process.

RTIC holds weekly meetings on Tuesdays at 19:00 CET in the project-dedicated Matrix chat room[6] and the meeting notes going back to late 2019 can be found at HackMD[7]. As of November 2020 the Matrix chat room has over 250 users. Not quite as many who has made `cortex-m-rtic` a favourite repository by giving it a star on GitHub[8], which as of writing this surpasses 550 users.

The meetings are meant to encourage interaction between members of the community and the core team, allow an informal way to report bugs and oddities, while at the same time letting the core team share what has happened since the last meeting in regard to *Action Points* and actual merged changes. Anyone can add to the meeting agenda and during the discussion points may be added if necessary.

The meeting is limited to 1 hour and someone from the core team will be moderating in order to keep from diving into general discussions better held outside of the designated meeting timeslot.

Besides the weekly meeting the Matrix chat act as a support and general RTIC discussion platform where both new and seasoned users can seek guidance from other community members and discuss anything related to RTIC and the surrounding tools and ecosystem.

The thought is that great ideas can be hatched during such discussion, leading to a RFC which then after being accepted becomes would become a GitHub issue. This issue will have one or more pull requests implementing the desired feature.

On 2020-06-11 during the review of the PRs for changing the name from RTFM to RTIC (section 4.3) I were invited to become a rtic-rs core team member.

With the invite came the ability to approve pull request and the responsibility to be a representative of the RTIC framework in the Matrix chat, handle bug reports and user submitted pull requests.

I consider this a nice experience, and the general atmosphere found within the RTIC community is truly welcoming and positive. It has been a great learning experience as well as an opportunity to teach embedded concepts to a broader audience interested in the subject. Additionally, with the gathered experience I feel more confident with state of the art software development procedures and tools available within the software industry.

The primary goal during this time has been to land all features destined to be part of release `v0.6.0` of the RTIC framework. This has been rewarding work, seeing many small parts combine into a potent framework for embedded Rust development.

The reception of the first alpha version[9] for the upcoming `v0.6.0` release was positive, some concerns were expressed about the need to always use the lock API for resources, but turns of the use-case was directly supported by using either of `#[task_local]` or `#[lock_free]`.

The sum of all changes

Some statistics gathered from the repositories, split by repository, see Figure 6.1 and Figure 6.2.

The count is for closed pull requests, except the last column which specifies the total number of GitHub Actions executed.

Total	Contributed	Reviewed	Tests
36	14	4	83

Figure 6.1: `rtic-syntax` pull request statistics

Total	Contributed	Reviewed	Tests
235	40	29	420

Figure 6.2: `cortex-m-rtic` request statistics

Refer to appendix A for more statistics about the changes implemented.

Figure A.3 Displays the `rtic-syntax` top contributors ranked by number of commits, also visible are the total cumulative sum of added and deleted rows. GitHub counts one changed line as one deleted row and then one re-added row.

Figure A.4 same as above but for the main repository `cortex-m-rtic`.

Figure A.5 if studying the overview of the RTFM organization the trend of the graphs tells an interesting story.

In the beginning many things are new and unfamiliar, but as time went more and more things became complete and after multi-core support was removed there has been an impressive amount changes, changes which were not attempted with multi-core present.

6.2 Usability and consistency

The first problem defined was the general concept of usability and consistency for the user interface. If the design is straightforward or even better, self-explanatory, less effort has to be spent during documentation and support.

With that in mind, the user facing syntax has seen improvements, especially in regard to how symmetrical interfaces reduce the likelihood of feeling lost and the amount of code needing change after a simple task priority change. If the method to achieve things are similar enough it becomes easier to remember and to focus on the finer details, such as the arguments to functions or name of attributes.

For the smallest possible RTIC example the syntax difference is also minimal. The module instead of const item implemented in `mod_const`[10] and the name change of RTFM can be seen in Listing 6.1 and Listing 6.2.

<hr>

```rust
//! examples/smallest.rs

#![no_main]
#![no_std]

use panic_semihosting as _; // panic handler
use rtfm::app;

#[app(device = lm3s6965)]
const APP: () = {};
```

Listing 6.1: RTIC v0.5.1 syntax of `examples/smallest.rs`

```rust
//! examples/smallest.rs

#![no_main]
#![no_std]

use panic_semihosting as _; // panic handler
use rtic::app;

#[app(device = lm3s6965)]
mod app {}
```

Listing 6.2: RTIC v0.6.0-alpha.0 syntax of `examples/smallest.rs`

The current list of changes to syntax and UI described in the development version of the RTIC framework book[11] under the migration chapter there is the procedure to convert a `v0.5.0` project to the to-be-released version `v0.6.0`.

The book is the primary source of documentation for the framework, easily accessible over at rtic.rs[12].

See appendix A for the full guide referenced above.

If asked to summarise all UI changes the answer would be: "symmetry".

- Task-local and lock-free
- Symmetric locks
- Symmetric interface for resources, init, idle, task

Other notable features not discussed in depth implemented primarily by me:

- `task_local` and `lock_free`[13] improves the ergonomics for resources either only shared by same priority tasks (`lock_free`) or by making the resource exclusive to just one task (`task_local`).

- Implement all clippy suggestions[14] fixes all issues Clippy could find.

There are other improvements not implemented by me personally, where I have acted reviewer. By discussing the pros and cons of the features with the core team and community one reaches good understanding of the features and the impact on the framework. These features listed are highly relevant to the furthering of the framework.

These changes will also be a part of the upcoming v0.6.0 release and there are some rather exciting ones.

- Implemented in v0.6.0-alpha.0

    - Spawn from anywhere[15] discussed in section 4.5, will allow greater flexibility in regard to spawning and scheduling tasks.
    - The bare_metal::CriticalSection[16] required by some HALs is now available.
    - Now late resources are always used[17] Makes the special init function symmetrical.
    - Dispatchers as app arguments[18] Removes the confusing extern section in favour of arguments to the macro.
    - Extern tasks[19] Allow calling RTIC tasks from outside of the mod app {}.

- For future alpha releases
    - New Monotonic implementation, support for multiple clocks
    - A way to cancel/reschedule scheduled software tasks

For a full list of desired changes before final v0.6.0 see this tracking issue[20].

6.2.1 Fear of Rust Macros

Fear is associated with what people are uncertain or unfamiliar with, the threat or danger being the uncertainty on how to handle that unknown challenge.

Rust macros are like any other technical challenge, there are a set of rules and it takes time to study and learn the "game".

The goal of the framework is to make it as easy as possible to go from idea to implementation, and while some concepts are easier than other the need to become an expert of Rust macros is not trivial.

From a user point of view the macros do something which is opaque and unknown, transforming the code, similarly to how the Rust compiler transform the rust code inte machine code. Since the Rust compiler is trusted to do "magic", one could reason that the framework also could reach this level where the underlying steps are abstracted away.

On the other hand, experienced developers may feel they loose oversight of their code, that the framework introduces needless complexity.

Both of these cases seems to boil down to the lack of insight into how the input gets transformed into output.

The framework outputs the generated code into target/rtic-expansion.rs which then can be studied to see what has been done. This can be useful during debugging and when the result is not as intended.

Another way to deal with the uncertainty is to make it fail proof enough that only the most special and unique use-cases need to go so far as to debug the macros.

With the continuously improved ergonomics of the Rust language the need for workarounds also disappears, see section 4.1.

There will always exist a use-case for metaprogramming, but with less noticeable indirection, as discussed in 1.3 Problem Definition, it may be more approachable.

6.2.2 Workarounds

The primary workaround which was resolved was `mod_const`. As visible in the following pull requests for rtic-syntax[21] and cortex-m-rtic[22] the changes implemented were not especially large in actual changed code the complexity came from fully understanding the Rust module system in combination with familiarising oneself with the codebase to begin with.

As discussed in section 4.1 the changes required much more than initially anticipated. This was due to some inconsistencies in the multi-core implementation causing the code generation to lack these symbols.

The decision was made to pause the development related to `mod_const` and instead focus on removing multi-core. After multi-core was successfully removed, see section 4.4, the almost complete `mod_const` implementation could be updated to match the new name, RTIC, of the project. Since all examples and tests has this fundamental construction many files needed attention, I value tools like `sd` and its forefather `sed` a lot.

6.3 Code Structure

The way a project structure the source code is dependent on many factors, it can be hard to find the "optimal structure" fulfilling every criteria because there are so many different use-cases and requirements. Thus the layout is often a compromise between different needs. Here the discussion focuses on the new goal of extensibility and the improvements made in order to realise this goal.

6.3.1 Modularity and implementation complexity

As indicated in section 4.5 the change of focus led to not implementing the desired change itself but the changes leading up to the next generation of the RTIC framework instead. The cause for this is that it was decided to try to simplify the structural complexity as much as possible before attempting to break it into smaller modular pieces. Then one change and improvement led to the other, with multi-core support gone the possible improvements seems never-ending thanks to the much leaner codebase and fewer special cases needed to be dealt with.

The overall code complexity has been greatly reduced as seen in section 5.5, but the code structure is similar to the previous structure as discussed in section 5.6.

To discuss the perceived complexity of the framework, a blog post by one of the members of stm32-rs[23] providing support projects for STM32 microcontrollers compares the various ways to achieve interrupt-driven code execution on embedded devices.

One of the concerns[24] listed for RTIC/RTFM is that in contrast to the other ways to develop software for Rust embedded, this was the least idiomatic. My interpretation of this statement is that the visibility and "clear" path between input and output is not as clear and elegant as Rust usually allows one to write, due to the Rust macro indirection.

The framework presents a Domain Specific Language (DSL) on top of regular Rust, which has its own set of keywords and UI elements to reach the desired functionality supported by the Rust ecosystem, LLVM compiler and a whole lot of other tools. With the asymmetric interfaces and special workarounds present in the version tested at the time of writing of the blog post, the UI would understandably appear as a bit inconsistent.

My hope is that with the recent improvements and general cleanup of the internal structure this will be less of an issue going forward.

Another negative was the feeling of extra implementation complexity even if all features of the framework are not in use. However, as noted in the epilog thanks to the impressive optimisations Rust and LLVM can do the final output is not affected by this complexity.

> As can be seen each of the approaches comes with a their own set of
> drawbacks and it would be great if there was a way to combine them in
> a way that combines the best of all worlds: The straight-forwardness of
> cortex-m with the simplicity of irq but the power, efficiency and compile
> time guarantees of cortex-m-rtfm.

> I think it comes down to preferences and willingness to rely on the guarantees
> provided by the tool, in this case a concurrency framework. It also depends on the
> use case, some tasks do not need a specialised tool, while other tasks do.

6.4 Continuous Integration

When I first started looking into the repositories and the tools supporting them a lot of it was new to me.

The UI and general impression of Travis CI, configured as it were, did not feel overly impressive. Yes it performed the job but it felt lacking, both in UI and performance.

Replacing Travis CI meant learning both the old and new ways of doing CI testing, and this I am sure will come in handy going forward within the field of software development.

The speed increase seen by optimising and changing to GitHub Actions makes a huge difference when working, more than once joy has been expressed by the core developers in relation to the swiftness of the new CI tool.

The change of CI was not initially motivated by the rumors of Travis CI having a change in direction regards their stance towards open-source, but rather the generally positive reception of GitHub Actions within the Rust embedded community. With the reasoning that the repositories themselves already are somewhat dependent on the GitHub infrastructure, further increasing this dependence to this same vendor does not seem as bad. Having multiple dependencies on multiple different vendors seems like more of a fragile setup due to the interdependencies, however the old and true idiom that one should not put all eggs in one basket still stands.

The acquisition by Idera caused a stir in the community, as seen in section 3.5. A recent development has however made even greater impact on the open-source projects depending on Travis CI.

Unfortunately the foreboding of the open-source community became reality. Jeff Geerling describes[25] it well, but here summarised:

2020-11-02 Travis CI announced that a new pricing model will be in place, limiting the open-source offering about 1000 minutes of testing time. As described in their FAQ[26] for public repositories:

> We will be offering an allotment of OSS minutes that will be reviewed and allocated on a case by case basis. Should you want to apply for these credits please open a request with Travis CI support stating that you'd like to be considered for the OSS allotment. Please include:
> - Your account name and VCS provider (like travis-ci.com/github/[your account name])
> - How many credits (build minutes) you'd like to request (should your run out of credits again you can repeat the process to request more or discuss a renewable amount)

By 2020-12-31 travis-ci.org[27] will become read-only, and all those who wish to continue using Travis need to migrate to the new travis-ci.com[28].

Chapter 7

Conclusions and Future Work

This chapter goes through conclusions made and then suggests future improvements.

7.1 Conclusions

Even though theoretical work has been presented for how to design a more extendable modular structure the implementation is not complete. The insight that to make such an overarching structural change, consensus within the community and primarily the core team, is required. To this end, in order to reduce the implementation complexity and thereby increase the chances of success it was deemed sensible to begin by spending effort on simplifying the code base by implementing the changes required for the RTIC framework to take a step towards the next release while furthering the standing of RTIC within the embedded community at the same time. Since some of these changes were in line with the changes needed for a new structural layout this changed the overall goal of this thesis.

Being a part of this Rust embedded open-source community has been a valuable experience, the general outlook and overwhelmingly positive response has further encouraged me to partake in such endeavours in the future.

On the other hand, driving change within a larger community takes more time compared to a solo project. In my opinion there is a happy medium, and the organisational structure the RTIC project employs seems to be achieving this by having a smaller core developer group steering the overall project, but still maintaining a strong bond with the community. With the help of the digital communication forums for both direct (Matrix) and more structured discourse (RFC, issues) the needs of the community can be gauged and work is often prioritised in order to solve the most frequently reported and discussed problems.

Thus everyone can contribute, even quick questions along the lines of "how do I do x with y, I have tried z" are an indication of an area where user documentation or usability in general might be lacking. Additionally, as the community grows the number of experienced users active in the Matrix chat room able to help newcomers also increase, thus the core developer group may find additional time focusing on other areas. By helping others and striving to improve both the framework and community is also a great way to earn a good reputation within the community itself.

The latest stable release version `v0.5.5` of `cortex-m-rtic` contains confusing user interface inconsistencies which often cause newcomers to doubt their abilities.

The released version `v0.6.0-alpha.0`[1] contains the cumulative improvements implemented during the work of this thesis. For both usability and general new or changed features. Together with `rtic-syntax` version `v0.5.0-alpha.0`[2] this allows for easier testing within the community where reception has been positive.

These improvements includes UI redesigns and usability fixes, mainly around the change towards a symmetric UI for both the `init` function and how to lock resources. Additionally, a new way to specify when to not have to lock resources has been implemented, supporting `#[task_local]` and `#[lock_free]` resources.

Improving the usability of the framework benefits both new and experienced developers, and with the ambition to enable everyone to build concurrent and deadlock free embedded systems, the user interface is as important as the correctness of the underlying execution model. However correct the model may be, if it is unusable it will not see wide adoption and usage. Additionally, a lacking user interface may risk discouraging new users since the time wasted wrestling with the unfamiliar and non-consistent syntax can be spent building embedded systems instead.

The state of the art Continuous Integration tools invaluable for software development have been discussed and compared.

Since a large part of the work done was in relation to furthering the RTFM/RTIC framework and governing the community, this thesis presents an account on how this work has improved the framework.

The largest changes bringing major improvements made as part of this thesis:

- Remove multi-core support, reduces overall complexity and increases maintainability
- Implement regular Rust modules instead of `const` pseudo-module workaround
- Replace Travis CI with GitHub Actions to reduce time required for test verification

For the details of all implemented changes for `cortex-m-rtic` see the full list of merged pull requests[3].

7.2   Future Work

Future work consists of reaching the desired feature set for releasing the stable version `v0.6.0`.

Before stable `v0.6.0` can be released more alpha-releases will be necessary, to properly verify all functionality and ensure that no part of the API will cause regret further on, in addition to letting the wider community test and provide feedback. With the release of `v0.6.0-alpha.0` a regression was discovered, user provided functions named `main` annotated with `#[task]` would conflict with the RTIC `main` required as a starting point of execution. Moving the RTIC `main` into a separate Rust module separates it from the RTIC `mod  app` module preventing conflict with the user provided function. Small details like these would be hard to test for without the varied and at times exotic use-cases provided by the community.

As the release of stable `v0.6.0` draws near the structure will be less volatile and the implementation of the proposed extendable structure can proceed.

Other features intended for the near future includes implementing support for
`embedded_time`[4], supporting multiple timers with a new `Monotonic` trait and changing the underlying storage model of the `heapless` data structure in order to support
a long awaited feature for canceling and rescheduling of scheduled software tasks.

A use-case could be having a task perform some action every 10 seconds in relation to the previous time that action were performed. A typical approach would
be to have a timer schedule this task for the future. If another action on the systems
triggers this task 5 seconds after it originally was run it would not be necessary to
run the task again just 5 seconds later. With this cancel and reschedule API it would
be possible to first cancel the scheduled invocation of the task, and then possibly re-
run the task setting up the scheduling of the task causing the new 10 second offset
to be counted from the current time.

`embedded-time` implements a library dealing with the notion of time on embedded systems making the interface with clocks[5] and durations[6] much more user
friendly.

On the more experimental side for future releases there is a lot of interest and
ongoing[7] work[8] to implement support for async/await and the RFC repository is full
of ideas.